Bully BUSTERS

A Teacher's Manual
for Helping Bullies, Victims, and Bystanders

Dawn Newman-Carlson

Arthur M. Horne

Christi L. Bartolomucci

Research Press ● 2612 North Mattis Avenue ● Champaign, Illinois 61822 ● (800) 519-2707 ● www.researchpress.com

To my mother and father: Your unwavering love and support have served as my foundation, a ground that keeps me stable even on the most turbulent of days. Thank you for taking part in my journey. Thank you for making my world complete.

—D. A. N.

To Lucy and Natalie: May the bullies of your life be few and far between.

—A. M. H.

To my parents, sisters, and Gav: Your love, courage, and support have served as my inspiration to embrace new opportunities and even the greatest of challenges.

—C. L. B.

Contents

Preface

In 1994, our research group at the University of Georgia received a request from a group of teachers at Clarke Middle School in Athens, Georgia, to assist in the development of a program to address the problem of bullying in their school. This manual is the result of our efforts. The teacher-based intervention program described here is one that evolved over time. Our first recommendation at Clarke Middle School was that they institute a comprehensive, schoolwide program modeled after other programs that had demonstrated to be effective (e.g., Olweus, 1978). Given the realities and resources of the Athens community, a large-scale effort of this kind was impractical for Clarke Middle School. Hence, we took a more cost-efficient and time-limited approach.

In this second, more limited approach, we considered the effectiveness of group counseling as a vehicle for change. We evaluated three kinds of groups: bullies only, victims only, and bullies and victims combined. Group counseling literature has long described homogeneous groups, or groups in which all members have the same presenting problem, as less effective than heterogeneous groups for helping bring about change, particularly for groups including aggressive children. It is better if the group represents a mixture of problems, particularly when aggression is a core element. This was the case with our own groups. The "bullies only" approach proved unsatisfactory because the bullies offered one another support in maintaining their aggressive behaviors. As a group, they identified the problem not as their own, but as the victims', who "deserved what they got."

Groups composed of victims only likewise proved unsatisfactory, for two main reasons. First, the victims wanted the bullies to change and saw it as unfair to expect those victimized to be the ones involved in the change process—they thought teachers and others should take responsibility for providing a safe environment, a position we supported as well. Second, victims made up a homogeneous group, one in which they all experienced the same problem and therefore supported one another in the belief that change could not occur.

A grouping combining both bullies and victims proved to be somewhat more effective than either of the two homogeneous groups. Teachers and group members reported that the groups were having a positive impact and that change was occurring. Unfortunately, when we conducted follow-up studies in which bullies and victims provided self-reports of the number of aggressive experiences they were involved with each day, we found no reduction in the level of bullying in the school.

As a result of our findings, we decided that group counseling, although a powerful intervention for dealing with many of the concerns and problems of middle school students, was not sufficient to bring about a change in the pattern of bullying and victimization of the children we studied. A more powerful intervention was necessary.

At this point, our emphasis changed from counseling with children to inservice training for teachers—the people who have the most direct contact with students and therefore the most opportunity to reduce bullying and victimization within the school. The results of more than 3 years of direct work with teachers have confirmed the power of classroom interventions to reduce the total level of bullying and victimization in schools (Newman, 1999; Newman & Horne, in press). We are now in our sixth year of work with teachers and other educators to prevent and reduce aggression in the school environment. We are finding that having educators who play an active role in their schools to change the culture are able to bring about a shift from a tacit endorsement of aggression to an environment in which there is a reduction of aggression and an increase in a sense of safety and personal acceptance. Both teachers and students report a greater sense of comfort at school, and reported aggressive acts are reduced.

The program described in this manual would not have evolved without the outstanding contributions of many people. First, we depend heavily on the more than two decades of excellent research and program development focusing on reducing violence and aggression in young people. We appreciate and acknowledge the outstanding contributions of those whose work provided the basis for our own applications: Gerald Patterson, Rex Forehand, Tom Dishion, Dan Olweus, Anthony Pellegrini, and Richard Hazler, among others.

We have also received exceptional support from the College of Education of the University of Georgia. The Office of the Dean has provided graduate assistant support for 5 years. The faculty and students of the Department of Counseling and Human Development, as well as of other departments, have contributed enormously to the program by volunteering time to conduct groups and by offering excellent suggestions for improving the program. In particular, the following faculty served on dissertation committees examining the bully reduction program: Brian Glaser, Georgia Calhoun, Rosemary Phelps, Pam Paisley, Richard Hayes, Jerry Gale, John Dagley, Jean Baker, Pamela Orpines, Richard Page, Steven Olejnik, Rex Forehand, Rog Martin, and Carl Huberty.

We would like to express our gratitude for the oustanding support and involvement of the teachers and administrators of Clarke Middle School. They participated in all aspects of the program, including identifying those children most in need, participating in the research, and providing feedback and recommendations for improvement throughout the entire life of the program. Rosemary Salter, school counselor, and Ken Sherman, principal, have given exceptional support and have encouraged continued program development and applications. We highly value their ideas and their continued work with school faculty to facilitate the program. Truly, this project exemplifies the successful effort to bridge the "town-gown" gap: The collaboration between faculty and students at the university and administrators and teachers at the school has been at the finest level.

An external evaluation of the program has been conducted in Ft. Wayne, Indiana. Our thanks to the trainer, David Jolliff, and to the teachers involved with this project. Natasha Howard and Ryan Scott completed the evaluation of the Ft. Wayne project. Preliminary results are highly supportive of the effectiveness of the program.

Our thanks also go to Ann Wendel, Russ Pence, Karen Steiner, and everyone else at Research Press for their their support, encouragement, and professional contributions. We appreciate their efforts in bringing this manual to publication and in helping the program reach a larger audience.

Although a systemic program of change involving everyone involved with the school and the educational process—teachers, administrators, students, parents, and community agencies—is plainly a potent intervention model, given the realities and resources available in most communities, we do not believe such programs are practical or will often be implemented. Fortunately, the more time- and cost-efficient focused approach described here can bring about significant change. We encourage you to join us in this process.

Introduction

School for many is not always the safe learning environment it was intended to be. Working against the sense of safety are the harsh realities of the bully/victim dyad, experienced by thousands of children every day. Many students are becoming increasingly anxious about witnessing bullying and increasingly fearful that they will be the next victims if they have not already been targeted (Olweus, 1978). In fact, bullying in schools has reached an alarming level, causing fear and concern for parents, their children, and the educators responsible for the safety of these children (Horne & Socherman, 1996).

Children are in school for a large portion of their lives and are in constant contact with teachers. This places teachers in a prime position to address bullying in the schools. The most effective ways teachers can manage the problem of bullying is by increasing their knowledge and awareness of the problem, ensuring that there are minimal opportunities for acts of bullying to materialize, and offering student support, training, and education aimed at attacking the root causes of bullying behavior (Besag, 1989). Unfortunately, many teachers feel helpless to address the problem of bullying due to a lack of adequate skills and training to intervene (Stephenson & Smith, 1989). Others fear that intervening in bullying situations will only "add fuel to the fire" and make the bullying worse. Because bullying often goes unnoticed and/or unattended by teachers, many students surmise that their teachers are unaware of these problems. Under this assumption, students often do not report them, creating a cycle in which this very real problem can easily be ignored by teachers, often exaggerating the problem.

It is essential that teachers be given the opportunity to learn about bullying and victimization, and that they be supported in their efforts to intervene. The program described here is designed as a collaborative effort in which teachers, support staff (counselors, social workers, psychologists, and others), and administrators can become more aware of the bullying problem and develop the knowledge base and skills to deal with the problem confidently. This manual serves as an educational guide as well as a classroom curriculum resource, providing information for teachers and others who have direct contact with students, as well as describing a number of classroom activities to increase students' awareness and encourage them to join in the process of change.

The approach outlined here emphasizes teachers' efforts toward both control and prevention of bullying behavior. The aim of control is to reduce occurrences of bullying, if not to eliminate them entirely; the aim of prevention is to induce conditions in which bullying is unlikely to occur in the future. Addressing the bullying problem openly, as we advocate here, can go a long way toward assuring students that their concerns really do matter and are worth bringing to their teachers' attention. Reaching these goals means a safer and more productive learning environment for everyone.

PROGRAM CONTENT

The program is organized as seven modules:

- **Module 1**   Increasing Awareness of Bullying
- **Module 2**   Recognizing the Bully
- **Module 3**   Recognizing the Victim
- **Module 4**   Taking Charge: Interventions for Bullying Behavior
- **Module 5**   Assisting Victims: Interventions and Recommendations
- **Module 6**   The Role of Prevention
- **Module 7**   Relaxation and Coping Skills

Teacher Information Component

Each module begins with a discussion for teachers of the particular topic. The modules are designed to give you a solid base of knowledge and to suggest issues that may be important for you to raise with your students. Following this material are a brief content review, along with prompts to use the Classroom Interaction and Awareness Chart, what we call "the Big Questions," and the Personal Goals Form. We will have more to say about these items later on in the introduction.

Classroom Activities

Each module includes three or four classroom activities. These activities correspond generally to the content of the module and are intended to increase student participation in efforts to reduce and prevent bullying, as well as to strengthen the teacher/student relationship. We encourage you to incorporate these activities into your regular lesson plans. In addition to the specific activities related to each module, we also urge you to review the additional classroom activities provided in Appendix A. Teachers have found these additional activities useful in sensitizing students to individual and cultural differences, encouraging empathy and communication, and enhancing students' receptivity to the antibullying message.

Processing the classroom activities is very important. In other words, once students are finished with the activity, it is important to spend time talking about their experiences of the activity itself. Typical processing questions elicit whether or not participants found the activity interesting, how involved they were, what they may have learned from it, and how they could use what they have learned in their lives outside the classroom and group. It is crucial for students to have the opportunity to discuss what they may have discovered about themselves or others during the process. Allow time for students to reflect and think, to consider the discussion questions and then apply the questions to themselves—this is the self-learning phase of the work. It is tempting to focus on the content, but the process in the activities is at least if not more important than the content.

Some students may have difficulty processing certain activities. For instance, the activity entitled "Framing the Bully," in Module 1, often results in increased understanding on the part of bullies of how others in the class perceive them. This learning experience is important, but it also can be disturbing. When talking with the class about bystander victims and the importance of helping victims of direct bullying, some students may feel guilty or self-conscious about their past failures to offer assistance. Be sensitive to the possible outcomes of the processing, and recognize that both pain and fulfillment may accompany learning.

If you are new to or unfamiliar with the group process, we encourage you to consider enlisting the help of an experienced co-leader when first doing the classroom activities, perhaps from a school counselor, psychologist, or social worker, or from another teacher who may be more experienced at group facilitation. That way the two of you can share the responsibilities for processing the group experience, and you can gain valuable feedback on your group skills.

PROGRAM IMPLEMENTATION

Three main options exist for implementing the program. First, program materials may be used by an individual teacher who wishes to increase students' awareness of bullying and improve conditions in her or his own classroom. Although a single committed individual can accomplish much, the other two options are more likely to succeed. In the second option, a group of school faculty elect to run the program as a team. Such a group may include any combination of teachers, school counseling or social work staff, other support staff, and administrators. Because of its broader base of support, this option reaches more students and is therefore more likely to result in change both in those individuals and in students and staff who, although not actively involved, experience the effects of the program indirectly. Broadest based and most effective of all is the third option, in which the program is integrated as part of the school curriculum and receives schoolwide support.

The Support Team

Regardless of how the program is implemented, we strongly encourage the establishment of Support Teams. The Support Team is a group of teachers and other staff who meet on a regular basis with the goals of mastering program content and providing a forum for mutual sharing and support. Each team generally includes from five to eight members. In addition to keeping teachers actively involved in working toward the goal of preventing and remediating school bullying, the team serves the following specific purposes.

Understanding and Clarification

Having a group of teachers preview the information and classroom activities makes it possible to discuss any questions about procedures or content.

Support

Teachers experience a level of encouragement and support by being able to share their encounters and feelings about their experiences.

Creativity

"The whole is greater than the sum of its parts" is true for programs such as this one. When Support Team members meet and develop plans, they expand upon the content in the manual and develop creative and exciting ways of using the material.

Problem Solving

The team can help each teacher analyze any ongoing problems that may develop, allowing for more effective problem solving.

The Support Team has been shown to be a powerful program component. In addition, we have found that working with a group makes the experience much more enjoyable and that, as a result, members are more likely to persist in their efforts.

Implementation by an Individual Teacher

If you are a teacher using the program independently in your own classroom, we recommend that you review all of the teacher information included in the modules, then select and engage students in the classroom activities you feel are best suited to your group. Even if you cannot create a formal Support Team, we urge you to seek out the aid of supportive colleagues. Making changes of this type is very difficult if you are "going it alone."

Implementation by a Group

The steps for a group of teachers and other school staff in forming a Support Team and mastering the program content are as follows.

Step 1: Select Team Members

Chances are you already have some kind of support group in place. Think of the colleagues you turn to when you are unsure of how to handle a situation or those who seek you out to request your assistance. Now take some time to solicit participation from at least five but no more than eight of your colleagues. If possible, try to encourage teachers from different grades to participate. A heterogeneous group of teachers is often beneficial because it allows teachers to share experiences along a grade-level continuum. Sharing experiences will help you prevent problems from happening in your classroom and assist others who are troubled by similar situations.

Step 2: Set a Time for the Team to Meet

In the beginning, the team should meet once a week, for 3 consecutive weeks, for approximately 2 hours each time. This time can be devoted to reviewing and discussing the different modules together, establishing plans to carry out the program, and deciding how to integrate the materials into the classroom curriculum. Following the first three meetings, the group should convene at least twice per month, for approximately an hour each time. We encourage you to seek out your fellow team members outside of meetings. When you need support or wish to share an experience with a fellow team member, do not wait for your next meeting. Keep in contact with your team members.

Step 3: Establish a Meeting Format

One thing I've learned about myself: left alone I get into a rut, but when our team met and I started hearing how others used the material, ideas just started popping into my head. Pretty soon I had so many new ways to handle the daily activities we were doing that I couldn't use them all. It was both surprising and exciting.

—Seventh-grade teacher

When I tried to figure it all out by myself and then work out all the steps, I was really intimidated. . . . When I listened to others discuss their being stuck, I got ideas on how to help with problems I had not even encountered yet. And it felt really good being able to help others—being a resource to the team.

—Sixth-grade teacher

It is important for the team to meet in an environment that is quiet and comfortable. Take turns bringing refreshments for your team. During the first three meetings, members will have an opportunity to become more familiar and comfortable with the program. Participants should be encouraged to share their knowledge, provide examples from their teaching experience, and suggest ways to introduce and integrate the materials in the classroom. We recommend that the group focus on Modules 1, 2, and 3 during the first meeting. These modules concern awareness of bullying and ways to recognize different types of bullying and victimization. During the second meeting, the emphasis is on Modules 4 and 5, interventions used with bullies and victims. The third meeting focuses on Modules 6 and 7, bullying prevention and coping strategies and skills to reduce stress. If your team is not able to cover the modules in the allotted time, you may decide to extend meeting times or perhaps add a fourth meeting.

After you have covered the module content, we strongly encourage you to begin holding meetings twice a month for an hour each time. We have found the following format for these meetings helpful:

1. At the start of each session, each member is encouraged to share briefly how the past few weeks have been and whether he or she needs some of the group's time to discuss bullying dilemmas, generate solutions to problems, share success or failure stories, or introduce an idea for a new classroom activity.

2. Once everyone has checked in, the floor is opened for discussion. Everyone who has expressed a need for a portion of the group's time is encouraged to share, starting with the first volunteer. When a member is sharing, the other members give feedback, provide suggestions, and share their own experiences. This process is likely to come very naturally to team members.

3. When there are about 10 minutes left in the hour, team members summarize the issues discussed. It is a good idea to review the same general questions at the end of each meeting (e.g., "What were the most helpful points addressed today?"; "In what areas are

people making progress?"; "What are some areas of concern?"; "What classroom activities have worked best?").

Step 4: Continue to Meet throughout the Year

If you are able to create a Support Team at the start of the school year, you will have the best opportunity to implement the program with the help of your colleagues. However, a late start is better than no start at all. Once you begin to meet, it is important for your team to meet consistently throughout the entire school year and beyond. We encourage you to continue to work as a team, perhaps adding new members, during subsequent years.

Schoolwide Implementation

Implementing the program on a schoolwide basis as part of the continuing education curriculum follows much the same procedures as the last option, implementation by a group. In this case, however, a workshop is the most efficient format for sharing the teacher information component of the program, and teachers form a number of Support Teams following the workshop. These teams follow the same guidelines described for implementation by a group: They include five to eight members and meet twice monthly for an hour each time to provide support, guidance, and collaborative problem solving.

In conducting educational workshops to cover the teacher information component of the modules, we have found the following procedures useful:

1. Make certain that everyone has a copy of this manual and has reviewed it prior to the first meeting.

2. The workshop/training sessions should convene once a week, over the course of 3 weeks, for 2 hours per meeting.

3. Teach the workshop curriculum in direct accordance with the manual. Doing so ensures that everyone has the same information at the end of the workshop.

4. During the first workshop meeting, cover Modules 1, 2, and 3. During the second meeting, devote attention to Modules 4 and 5. During the third, teach Modules 6 and 7. Each workshop should follow the same instructional format, combining both didactic and experiential approaches. The didactic part includes presenting and discussing the content of the module. The experiential component involves discussing how each participant may use the material, role-playing or practicing the steps to be taken, giving helpful corrective feedback so participants may practice and improve their skills, and acting out the material so teachers will have good familiarity with each module.

5. When the content has been covered, divide teachers into separate Support Teams, each including from five to eight members. Again, groups that are heterogeneous bring more diversity, allowing

broader problem solving and creativity. It is also important for group members to work well together so friendships may contribute to group cohesion. Members selected across grades can help one another identify and practice responses to the types of bullying problems shown at different levels. The most important factors are a willingness to work together on the problem and a collaborative relationship.

Following the workshop, teachers often question the reasoning behind participating in a Support Team. They ask, "Does this mean the workshops are insufficient to promote change in teachers' knowledge and intervention skills, and in students' bullying behaviors?" The answer is YES. In fact, research stresses the importance of combining educational workshops and follow-up support groups, indicating that of teachers in inservice training workshops, those who participate in follow-up groups supporting the use of workshop skills use the skills more often and more effectively in the classroom (Shapiro, DuPaul, Bradley, & Bailey, 1996). The degree to which your efforts are effective stems largely from your motivation to continue meeting and working together as a team.

EVALUATION

Evaluation is an essential component of any intervention to change attitudes and behaviors. At the end of the teacher information component of each module, it is important to ask yourself the following questions, by way of an informal evaluation of your readiness to proceed with classroom activities:

- Have I reviewed the material and do I understand the concepts well enough to begin implementing them in my classroom?

- Have I met with my Support Team to discuss the main points of the module and practiced my presentation so that I'm comfortable talking with my class about the subject?

- Have I reviewed the classroom activities we are going to do and made sure I have the materials and understand the concepts being presented?

After completing the classroom activities and related discussion, assess your effectiveness in reaching students: Do the students seem to understand the material? Are they supporting the bully-reduction plan? It is important to gauge students' responsiveness to the material in the very first module. If you are not experiencing the success you would like, take time to problem-solve and identify ways to improve the process. In evaluating students' responses, it is important to remember that many of the program's concepts are new, and if students are not entirely supportive or understanding, this may be at least partly because the topics are unfamiliar, sometimes even stressful. At the same time, changes in students' attitudes and willingness to discuss bullying incidents with you and one another should be evident.

Estimates of change can aid you in improving your delivery of the program, help students identify improvements in their peer interactions and level of security at school, and give parents, administrators, and other school staff information about the program's impact. Three items are helpful in this regard: the Teacher Inventory of Skills and Knowledge (TISK), the Classroom Interaction and Awareness Chart (CIAC), and the Personal Goals Form.

Teacher Inventory of Skills and Knowledge

Before you begin the program, we ask that you photocopy and complete the Teacher Inventory of Skills and Knowledge (TISK), given as Appendix B in this manual. Appendix C gives a Scoring Menu and Scoring Summary for this inventory. This inventory was developed to assess your knowledge and use of skills in each of the areas covered in the seven program modules. We will ask you to complete the TISK before beginning the modules, then return to it several times as you read and work to implement the program. We encourage you to complete the TISK at the end of each module to see how you are progressing, as well as at the end of Module 7 to evaluate your mastery of all the modules. In addition, during the school year it is good to complete the TISK periodically to evaluate whether "slippage," or a gradual drift away from using the skills, has occurred.

Classroom Interaction and Awareness Chart

The TISK is designed to assess overall knowledge at specific points during the program; the Classroom Interaction and Awareness Chart (CIAC) allows you to keep a running log of the bullying incidents you observe and your responses to them. It is best to complete the log daily, as incidents occur. Some teachers record only the incidents they observe directly, but others also record events students or others report to them. Reviewed periodically, the information you gather can give you an idea of the frequency of bullying events, insight into which students are involved and what circumstances may be supporting such behaviors, and a general sense of the direction of change. Your record does not have to be greatly detailed, but it should include enough information so you can recall what occurred, even several months in the future. A sample CIAC is provided on the next page; a blank copy of the chart is provided in Appendix D. In the sample, students are identified by their initials. A student number could also be used to preserve confidentiality.

Personal Goals Form

The Personal Goals Form is a separate page included at the end of each module. It serves as a place for you to record your plans to integrate the information in a way that relates to your own situation. Specifically, it lists the module goals and gives you the opportunity to describe what behaviors relating to the module content you observe in the classroom,

CLASSROOM INTERACTION AND AWARENESS CHART

Week of: _____ 3/20

DATE	LOCATION/TIME	STUDENT(S)	BEHAVIORS	INTERVENTIONS
1/15	Classroom (Period 3)	PM	Shoving incident	Told student to sit down and keep his hands to himself.
1/15	Classroom (Period 4)	RT	Entered class teary-eyed with head down	Inquired why: RT said he was hit in the hall.
1/16	Bus area, after school	DN	Saw DN walk by several students, knocking books out of hands.	Pulled student aside. Had her apologize.
1/16	Classroom	BJ, NT	BJ reported being threatened by NT. He said NT was going to hit him after class.	Talked to both BJ, NT.
1/17	Lunchroom	SN	Saw SN trip PJ in the lunchline.	Sent SN to the office.

identify activities you will conduct with students and how you will give them feedback, and record what type of communication you plan with your colleagues. It is recommended that you photocopy the Personal Goals Form for each module, then, as you read the teacher information portion of each module, keep the Personal Goals Form for that module handy to record your thoughts.

PERSPECTIVES ON THE LEARNING PROCESS

We try to teach a number of things when we conduct workshops with teachers interested in implementing the program. One of the first is that bullying is a form of aggression. Aggression and violence have become epidemic as a problem facing educators today. Our goal is to reduce or, preferably, eliminate entirely, all forms of violence and aggression in the schools. Since the program began in 1994, we have attempted to identify specific attitudes, beliefs, and orientations that are useful for teachers in their efforts to reduce bullying and victimization in their classrooms. We have found that a shift in our way of thinking is critical to the success of interventions based on the modules. The following sections suggest different ways of thinking about ourselves as change agents and about the problem itself. These perspectives allow us to help students in more positive and exciting ways.

Setting Up for Success

In our own teaching and in our work with teachers, we sometimes encounter situations where people seem to be "stacking the deck" against themselves. They take on tasks too big, address problems that can't be remedied in the school setting, or attempt to do their work in the way they always have, even when that way does not work anymore. Other times they may be required to tackle problems for which they have too little training or experience, and they become frustrated as a result. Setting up for success implies that we should actively plan to be successful. To do this, it helps if we know certain things about ourselves and the process of learning and change.

Prevention Beats Intervention

It is always better to prevent a problem than it is to treat it after it has happened. Two metaphors are helpful in bringing this idea to life.

The Lifeguard versus the Swim Teacher

It is important to have lifeguards to save the lives of children who are in trouble in the water. It is equally important to have instructors to teach children to swim so they do not require the help of a lifeguard. Both roles are important, but the preventive approach avoids the risk and trauma associated with having one's life in danger.

The Mechanic versus the Gardener

Mechanics fix things that are broken—they attend to problems and try to repair damage. Gardeners enjoy helping plants grow, providing the nurturing environment they need. J. Jeffries McWhirter says, "Rather than the hasty tinkering of the mechanic, nurturing life requires the patience of the gardener. The fast technological rush of society leads us to be mechanics. We must preserve the long patience of the gardener" (McWhirter, McWhirter, McWhirter, & McWhirter, 1998, p. 3). We believe teachers should work as gardeners, nurturing and tending to the development of healthy children. This eliminates the need for fixing problems later on. The prevention and early intervention approaches— rather than therapeutic treatment after the fact—pay great dividends.

By studying the problems we have in classrooms, we can often predict the future, in that we know what types of situations lead to problems of aggression and violence. In behavioral terms, knowing the ABC's is important, where A = the antecedent, B = the behavior, and C = the consequence. Knowing what antecedents or situations lead to bullying behavior in the classroom or school environment and then altering those situations so that the bullying doesn't happen in the first place is easier than fixing the problem once it has erupted.

If you observe carefully, can you begin to identify what the circumstances are before bullying situations occur? Are there predictable patterns? Can steps be taken to change these situations—the antecedents—before the aggression is realized?

Know What You Can Influence or Change

As part of our work with teachers and other school staff to develop programs to address bullying problems in their schools, we ask teachers to identify the problems the school faces. Once problems are identified, we list causes of or influences on the problems. If, for example, bullying is a problem, we attempt to identify what causes or influences the bullying. This may include poor anger control on the part of the students, parents who spend too little time with children, and violence in TV and movies. We then ask teachers to rank the causes, from highest to lowest, according to what they believe to be the most and least important influences on bullying behavior. Participants then rank the problem areas in terms of the degree to which they can be changed—from problems that can be influenced readily, such as anger control in the classroom, to those over which there is little influence, such as violence in movies. We then develop a quadrant and place the items in the quadrant along an x axis (How important is the issue?) and along a y axis (How much influence do you have?). This results in a figure like the one on the next page.

After identifying situations over which teachers have little or no influence, we ask how much energy they think we should spend in our program addressing these problems. That is, if we are attempting to set ourselves up for success, how much effort should we devote to areas over which we have absolutely no, or very little, influence, such as vio-

	Not very important	Very important
Considerable influence	Laughing in the bathroom Whispering in class	Sexual harassment Fighting in class Name-calling Teasing
Little influence	Teasing a neighbor's dog TV watching on weekends	High rate of violence in child's neighborhood Lack of family cohesion Lack of family support for schooling

lence in the movies? We then refocus our energies on those areas over which we do have influence: those in the school and the classroom. We also examine problems we cannot change directly but that may be amenable to our influence, such as parent involvement. It quickly becomes clear that spending lots of energy on areas over which we have no influence is setting up for failure, not success.

Rearrange the Environment

Our physical surroundings impact how we behave. If you examine the classroom itself, are there ways to rearrange the room so that it is less conducive to bullying or other disruptive behavior? If you know, for example, that certain students are likely to engage in bullying behavior and that other students are likely to be targeted, can the seating arrangement early in the year separate these students? Do you have transitions in your classroom, like beginning assignments or shifting from discussion to seatwork activities, that are conducive to aggressive acts such as pushing or teasing? Can those transitions be managed differently so there is less likelihood the problem will develop? One teacher brought wind chimes to her class. At each transition, she rang the chimes and told students they had until the chimes were quiet to be ready for the next activity. The students lowered their voices so they could keep on hearing the chimes, becoming quieter and quieter in the process.

Establish Clear Classroom Rules

Generally, teachers do not like to have a long list of "do's" and "don't" in their classrooms because the mood created by such a list is one of distrust, challenge, and confrontation. On the other hand, it is important early in the school year to establish classroom procedures and guidelines for behavior. Although each teacher elects a different level of rule setting at the beginning of the year, a universal expectation is that all members of the school community will treat one another with respect and dignity. The guideline of interpersonal respect is very important to establish early on. Later, as incidents arise, it is then possible when problems occur to return to this theme with a response such as "You recall that in our classroom we show respect for one another. Name-calling and teasing are not respectful. What can you do that will show respect?"

Be Consistent

The students with whom we have worked—bullies, victims, and bystanders—all have a strong sense of justice. We often hear students complain, "It just isn't fair." One way teachers can avoid being pulled into the fairness quagmire is by being consistent in the way they treat children. To allow one child to misbehave then reprimand another for the same behavior will invariably be seen as unjust. If the rule fits, it should fit all. In our efforts to reduce misbehavior in the classroom, it is important for teachers to model the characteristics they want from their students, and consistency in showing respect and treating one another with dignity is an essential characteristic.

Avoid Public Confrontations

We most often become aware of bullying behavior in a public setting—the classroom, playground, lunchroom, hallways, and so forth. It is important to stop the bullying behavior at once. At the same time, it is better to move toward remediation and change in a more private setting. Attempting to change bullying behavior in the public forum puts the student on the spot in terms of having to defend or explain. The student may react negatively to avoid losing face for being "dissed" by a teacher in front of peers. Public confrontations can lead to an escalation of emotions and aggression, neither of which is conducive to positive change. A teacher might say, for example, "Robert, stop that now. The rule is no name-calling or teasing. I'll talk with you back in the classroom before the others come in about how we are going to handle this. Now continue with your lunch."

It is almost never a good idea to get into a public power struggle with a bully. Engaging in a power struggle is likely to escalate the conflict, and the student may refuse to yield or resort to increased aggression. All children need an "out," a way to step aside from an awkward situation. In a public forum it is difficult for the teacher to help the student find a graceful way out of conflict.

Use Clear, Polite, Specific Language

We encourage teachers to "say what you mean, and mean what you say." This recommendation is aligned with the goal of consistency and fairness, discussed earlier. Our experience in classroom situations is that when a teacher says students are expected to behave in a particular way, it is important to follow through with the stated consequences, whether positive or negative. If the teacher doesn't require students to behave as requested, the students learn that the teacher doesn't mean what he or she says. They then begin to test the limits to see how far they can push the teacher before they will be reined in.

In communicating with students, teachers need to be very clear and specific. A general statement such as "I want all students to behave in my classroom" does not communicate what is expected. The statement "I want you to sit at your desks until you have finished this assignment, then you may do quiet work at the study table in the back of the room" is quite clear. Say what you want, when you want it, how you want it. Often in working with aggression in the classroom it is necessary to move closer to the student, establish eye contact, speak to the student by name, and wait for acknowledgment that you have been heard.

Language used with students also must be polite. If we expect students to demonstrate respect for one another, we will need to model that respect in our language with students. It is important for the tone of voice to be firm and polite, not sarcastic, critical, or punitive.

When working with students who are aggressive, it also is usually a good idea to "own" your part of the issue under discussion, rather than attribute your expectations to the student. You could say, for example, "I need you to take a seat now, away from Sean," rather than "Don't you want to take a seat now?" The latter question provides the opportunity for the student to answer, "No, I don't want to." Expressing what you want and need as your issue, rather than the student's, helps avoid escalating conflict.

Teach New Skills

Part of setting up for success is accepting that many of the students in our classes lack the skills necessary to carry on the peer relationships we would like to see. If students don't have the skills, or if the skills they have are inappropriate, then it becomes our responsibility to incorporate skill development into our instruction. To do this, we need to evaluate what skills students have, what the current skill level may be, and what additional skills need to be learned. We then need to provide the opportunity for students to learn them. Although some academic courses do not lend themselves to teaching prosocial skills, many do, and we can generally afford a few minutes of each day to provide learning opportunities. Students will learn better the younger they are and the more the skills are part of their daily living and learning. Although the content of our subject matter is very important, it is also important to be aware that as adults people are much more likely to lose jobs as a result of poor interpersonal problem solving than as a result of not being able to name the signers of the Declaration of Independence.

Take Care of Yourself

We have had a number of teachers indicate, when starting the program, that they feel burned out on teaching. This feeling is often presented as a function of the types of students they have in their classrooms. Our experience is that teachers don't burn out from too much teaching;

burnout occurs when teachers do not feel successful in their work. We all know people who put in very long hours on projects—long distance runners who run marathon after marathon, musicians who practice and play endless hours, teachers who remain energized year after year. People burn out when they no longer feel good about their efforts. It happens when needs—personal and emotional—are no longer being met by what we are doing.

Teachers enter the profession because of their love of teaching and working with young people. When their energy is drawn away to address bullying and other forms of aggression, there is less time for teaching. And when teachers feel ill-prepared to address the bullying problem, they become even more frustrated.

It is important for teachers to stay healthy and experience a sense of well-being. A teacher is a professional, and personal growth is important and must be built into any attempt to help students change. The last module of this book provides stress-relieving and energy-restoring activities. While you are providing numerous services for your students, you must remember to take care of yourself. In addition, your students can benefit from the classroom activities in this module, designed to help them relax, manage stress, and cope.

Using the "Act NICE" Approach

So much of school culture is "problem focused"—that is, the focus is on the problems teachers encounter. In the considerable time we have spent in schools, we have heard extensive discussion about problems, the diagnosis of problems, and strategies to stop problems. However, the problem focus puts the emphasis on what is wrong, on what students can't do, and generally leads teachers to feel frustrated and exasperated, feelings that often lead to a sense of hopelessness and sometimes to giving up.

A focus on solutions rather than problems subtly changes the beliefs and expectations we have about our students. Because a solution-focused approach views both students and schools as being capable of change and improvement, it helps us become more optimistic about the outcomes of our work with students. Focusing on strengths and positive changes encourages students and teachers to build expectations for success. Central to the solution-focused approach are the following assumptions.

Bullying and victimization derive from a mismatch between the competencies of the student and the demands of the classroom and school environment

Having effective social skills represents a high level of cognitive and behavioral development for students. Many students come from situations where models of prosocial behavior have been inadequate and opportunities to observe appropriate peer and adult interactions few. In many families today, effective bonding or attachment to significant adults has not occurred, resulting in an inability on the part of some students to be empathic and/or able to take others' perspectives. If a student has not learned effective empathy skills—understanding how others feel—then he or she will be unable to care about whether others are hurt or offended. Focusing on the "why" of the lack of empathy is a problem-focused approach and does not help us bring about desired behaviors in the school situation. If we are solution focused instead, we become able to look for ways to teach our students the skills we seek: We focus on the "how"—how to help students become more socially skilled—rather than on why students lack skills.

Teachers are experts

Teachers are experts with students and their subject matter. They work with hundreds of students and understand child development, curriculum planning, individual learning styles, and classroom management. Teachers are the "front line" of educating and caring for students, the ones who have taken on the responsibility for helping students move through the tumultuous periods of their lives as they attempt to master the academic skills they need for the future as well as develop the core relationship skills that will so powerfully influence their lives in the years to come.

Many barriers get in the way of teachers' ability to work creatively toward solutions for their students

The world of the teacher today is one of too little time to individualize instruction, a shortage of resources, ever-increasing class sizes, low parental support, and, oftentimes, increased demands from school boards, administrators, or legislators for greater productivity. Today's teachers need support and encouragement to handle the myriad expectations placed upon them. Some of the problems teachers experience can be managed by other professionals outside of the classroom: special education classes for children with severely disruptive behavior or special learning needs, counseling for those with emotional needs that cannot be met within the classroom structure, and alternative schools for those whom the public school environment truly does not fit. Still, the main responsibility for teaching and change is held by classroom teachers. They have the commitment and experience to be powerful influences in the lives of students. Giving teachers the specific skills to intervene with bullies and victims empowers them to be even more influential in bringing about change.

"Act NICE" is a specific solution-focused approach to solving classroom problems. It allows both teachers and students to think positively about students' ability to learn and to use appropriate prosocial behaviors in school. This approach helps ensure student success; it also gives teachers a greater sense of control over their interactions with students. *NICE* stands for *Notice, Increase, Create,* and *Encourage.* The components of the approach are as follows.

N = Notice

Notice that even bullies don't always act aggressively—and victims are not always victimized. At times, in fact most of the time, bullies and victims do quite well. Our job is to notice when, where, with whom, and under what conditions the problems are not occurring and bullies and victims are, in fact, behaving appropriately. The process requires that we focus on what we want students to be doing instead of the problematic behavior (the solution, rather than the problem) and then notice what is happening when the appropriate behavior is occurring.

I = Increase

When we have figured out what circumstances seem to result in bullies not bullying, victims not being victimized, then we need to increase the circumstances in which those events occur. In other words, we need to do more of what already works. When the bully is engaged in prosocial behavior rather than bullying, then the bullying is nonexistent. In other words, increasing prosocial behavior automatically decreases bullying. In addition, positive interactions can themselves become reinforcing and result in a decrease in bullying.

C = Create

Creative thinking on the part of teachers can lead to opportunities for bullies and victims to experience more prosocial and positive interactions, at the same time reducing the aggression and violence that generally has been our focus. Finding new ways to engage students in positive discussions, encouraging them to share in supportive tasks, and helping them discover alternative ways of being all call for creative thinking. When teachers work creatively with one another, sharing their ideas on how to find solutions to common problems and supporting one another in addressing unique situations, they create an environment that looks for solutions. (One specific way we nurture creativity is by asking ourselves the Big Questions, discussed next.)

E = Encourage

Encourage and celebrate successes—even small ones. Use descriptive statements rather than evaluative praise to let students know what they are doing right. For example:

- Jeremy, you and Fletcher looked like you were on a collision course but seemed to settle it quickly and in a friendly way. Thanks.

- Martha, I noticed you were including Heather in the group work you were doing. That is really good—thanks for being so considerate.

Using problem-solving, rather than problem-finding, language encourages students to think about solutions:

- Does name-calling support our class rule about showing respect for others? (Rather than "Stop name-calling.")

- What do you think we need to do to resolve this problem? (Rather than "Let me tell you what you need to do.")

Asking the Big Questions

We find that rather than dwell on what is wrong and "awfulizing" ourselves into being down and despondent, it is more helpful to examine what *is* working, then work toward solutions. What we call the "Big Questions" help us to do that:

1. What is my goal?

2. What am I doing? (identifying the problem)

3. Is what I am doing helping me achieve my goal? (focusing on solutions)

4. *(If not)* What can I do differently? (generating options)

Once we choose an option and try it out, we can evaluate whether our solution is helping us achieve the goal we identified for ourselves. If not, we can generate and try out new options until we find a workable solution.

We use the Big Questions extensively, with our students and with ourselves. When used with a student, the first question is designed to help the student stop doing what he or she has been doing and to examine what his or her goals may be. Generally, teachers discuss academic and interpersonal goals with students at the beginning of the year (as part of the process of setting up for success, described previously). Some of the interpersonal goals may be developing friendships, getting along with others, or being respected by and showing respect for others. Often students can't answer the question "What is your goal?" and so we answer it for them. In fact, we often skip over this question and provide the answer as we move to the second question, "What are you doing?" A dialogue between teacher and student might sound like the following, for example. Note how the teacher moves toward solutions in a supportive and encouraging manner.

Teacher: Sean, your goal is to get respect and be respectful. What are you doing now?

Sean: Nothing.

Teacher: Sean, you were calling Ryan names. Does that show respect?

Sean: No, but he was calling me names, too.

Teacher: So if calling names doesn't show respect or get respect, is there something you can do differently?

Sean: I don't know. Maybe.

Teacher: Good, let's talk about what else you might do. I'm sure we can come up with something different. Let's talk about what that might be.

We often print the Big Questions on business-size cards, then laminate them and have students carry the cards with them in their pockets. When in a conflict, students can then pull out their cards and read through the Big Questions to help them find a way to deal with the situation. (We keep extra copies because the cards often go through the washing machine!) We have had parents call and request copies for all their family members and even report that the questions have been useful for helping them problem-solve at work instead of saying, "Take this job and shove it."

We strongly suggest that you ask yourself the Big Questions frequently as you work through the program modules. Everyone's answers will be different. To illustrate what we mean, however, we offer the following example. The teacher in this case is asking the Big Questions just before beginning this program.

Question: What is my goal?
Answer: To be the most effective, helpful, and influential person I can in the lives of the students with whom I work.

Question: What am I doing?
Answer: I am attempting to provide the best learning experiences I can but at times feel overwhelmed because I do not know what to do to help the students who are less powerful and who are picked on by other students.

Question: Is what I am doing helping me achieve my goal?
Answer: No, I have been looking the other way, ignoring bullying incidents, and wishing they would all go away. Sometimes I am miserable because I dislike both the bully and the victim and don't know what to do about either one.

Question: What can I do differently that will help me achieve my goal?
Answer: I can focus clearly on the modules presented in this text and study them, share some ideas on how to use them with my fellow teachers, and begin using the activities with my class. I need to set aside a period of time each day (say, 15 minutes) to study the materials and think about how to incorporate them into my teaching.

A FINAL WORD

As you increase your awareness of bullying problems and become more sensitive to the issues involved, you may feel that the problem of aggressive behavior is inevitable and beyond your control. It may seem that things are getting worse instead of better. Hang on! Stay encouraged, for becoming aware of the problem is the first step toward improving your classroom environment and decreasing bullying interactions. Although some issues may be new to you, you can be sure your students have been dealing with them for quite some time. It is important to remain dedicated and continue to offer support to your students. Things will get better.

We believe mastering the information and using the classroom activities in this manual will allow you to devote more time to your teaching and empower you as you become more accomplished in your management of both bullies and victims. We know teachers' schedules are very busy! However, the time you devote to the program now will pay off in fewer problems and more time for teaching later.

Up to this point, we have made a number of recommendations for using the program materials, but we hope you will adapt the program to your own situation and use the materials creatively. Introduce your ideas to your team. This is your time. Make it worth your while. Don't hesitate to ask for what you need. And, most important, remember you are not alone in handling your bullying dilemmas: You have team support.

Now we encourage you to get started!

Before You Begin...

Take a moment to photocopy and complete the Teacher Inventory of
Skills and Knowledge (TISK), given as Appendix B. Be as open and
honest about answering the questions as you can so this information
will be an accurate preassessment of your knowledge of the information
in this manual. Once you have completed the inventory, score it by
using the Scoring Menu and Scoring Summary in Appendix C. Set the
TISK and its scoring forms aside, then go on to Module 1.

MODULE

1 Increasing Awareness of Bullying

OVERVIEW

School attendance is required in all of our United States. It is important for students to go to school in a safe and supportive environment, and teachers are primarily responsible for helping make that happen in their classrooms. Teachers are active change agents—in fact, their specialty is changing what young people know and what they can do. We easily accept the importance of helping students change with regard to their knowledge and even other behaviors (e.g., through such activities as physical education and sports). It is crucial that we expand our understanding of our role to include changing behaviors of students that result in fear and intimidation on the part of other students. The first step in tackling bullying in your school is to understand what constitutes bullying and determine its prevalence in your classroom. Many teachers find it difficult to define bullying and are unsure how they can help. This module will help you understand the problem of bullying as well as assist you in establishing conditions to prevent and reduce bullying in your classroom.

GOALS

- To become aware of the scope of the bullying problem
- To understand and apply the "Double I/R" criteria for bullying
- To develop a personal definition of bullying
- To identify teachers' role in the prevention and remediation of bullying
- To learn the core conditions for reducing bullying and victimization

SCOPE OF THE PROBLEM

I know a lot about bullies. I know they have a specific social function: they define the limits of acceptable conduct, appearance, and activities for children. They enforce rigid expectations. They are masters of the art of humiliation and technicians of the science of terrorism. They wreaked havoc on my entire childhood. To this day, their handprints, like a slap on the face, remain stark and defined on my soul. (Rofes, 1994, p. 37)

As Eric E. Rofes so poignantly notes, the impact of bullying on a single victim can be profound. Bullying affects many children around the world. Every day thousands of children are physically or psychologically abused in their school environment. Did you know . . .

- 285,000 students are physically attacked in school each month (Batsche & Knoff, 1994).

- 89% of respondents from over 700 cities confirmed that violence in the schools was a problem in their communities (Arndt, 1994).

- 160,000 children miss school each day because of fear (Lee, 1993).

- 70% of students have experienced bullying at some point in their academic careers (Hoover, Oliver, & Hazler, 1992)

- 14% of students believe that the exposure to bullying has a severe impact on their lives (Hoover et al., 1992).

Many teachers have questions about what actually constitutes bullying. After years of examining the phenomenon, researchers have isolated some common themes in the relationship between bully and victim. Following are several definitions found in the bully/victim literature.

> Bullying should be seen on a continuum of severity. The term *bullying* is all embracing including anti-social acts such as assault, extortion, intimidation, and violence. Bullying is a willful, conscious desire to hurt another person. (Tattum, 1989, p. 10)

> A student is being bullied or victimized when he or she is exposed, repeatedly and over time, to negative actions on the part of one or more other students. . . . It is a negative action when someone intentionally inflicts, or attempts to inflict, injury or discomfort on another. (Olweus, 1994, p. 1173)

> A student is being bullied or picked on when another student says nasty and unpleasant things to him or her. It is also bullying when a student is hit, kicked, threatened, locked inside a room, sent nasty notes, and when no one ever talks to him. These things can happen frequently and it is difficult for the student being bullied to defend himself or herself. It is also bullying when a student is teased repeatedly in a nasty way. (Smith & Sharp, 1994, p. 1)

Bullying is long-standing violence, physical or psychological, conducted by an individual or a group, and directed against an individual who is not able to defend himself in the actual situation. The physical bullying could include kicking, pushing, or beating the victim, while the most common means of psychological bullying are teasing and exclusion. (Roland, 1989, p. 143)

As the last two observers point out, bullying behaviors extend beyond physical abuse and violence to include psychological intimidation—behaviors such as verbal abuse, threats, teasing, and intentional exclusion from group activities. In fact, bullying in the form of verbal abuse is quite prevalent, for it is more likely to occur without attracting the attention of school personnel.

THE "DOUBLE I/R" CRITERIA FOR BULLYING

Despite the existence of "expert" opinions, teachers often find it difficult to determine what does and does not constitute bullying. One way to clarify the situation is to use the "Double I/R" criteria. As the name implies, bullying behavior is *intentional, imbalanced,* and *repeated.*

Intentional

Bullying incidents are not accidental. Rather, the bully intends to inflict harm upon the victim. We often see incidents where one child may cause harm to another through exuberance or overactivity. This may be the case, for example, when a student with Attention Deficit/Hyperactivity Disorder (AD/HD) becomes disruptive and hurts someone without intending to do so, later expressing remorse. Bullying also differs from typical childhood play in that children who commit bullying behaviors intentionally inflict injury or discomfort on another individual. "Rough-and-tumble" play is common on playgrounds as well as in lunchrooms, hallways, and other places. Although rough-and-tumble play can escalate into aggression—even bullying—generally, it does not. Most kids do not intentionally hurt other kids, and the peer group usually serves as a balance to ensure that normal play does not escalate into either aggression or bullying. In rough-and-tumble play, when one person wants to stop or expresses that what is happening hurts, the other person stops. In bullying, the behavior continues or even escalates.

Imbalanced

Bullying occurs in an interpersonal relationship characterized by an imbalance of power, physical or psychological. Bullies are adept at identifying other students who lack the skills, abilities, or personal characteristics to defend themselves. In brief, bullies are masters of the abuse of power and use of coercion.

Repeated

To be considered bullying, the acts must not only reflect intention and an abuse of power, they must also occur more than once. It is when incidents are repeated and beyond the control of the victim that bullying is occurring and teachers must step in to provide support and protection. "Single-event" acts of aggression are certainly problematic and require our attention. Most students experience the occasional unpleasant or even aggressive act in school but are able to handle the incident. The suggestions in this manual for intervening with bullies, victims, and bystanders will work to reduce single-event aggression, too, but our focus is on the repetitive attacks of bullies on victims.

Each of the following scenarios describes a situation that occurs commonly in schools. As you read through them, consider the "Double I/R" criteria. Which scenarios constitute bullying? How do these incidents of bullying differ from typical childhood play? If you are like most teachers, you probably have witnessed events similar to these in your classroom. How would you address each of these situations?

SCENARIO 1

Brenda is a sixth grader whose body is maturing much faster than that of other girls her age. She is embarrassed about her development and often walks down the hall with her books covering her chest. Brenda's classmates, along with other students at school, poke fun at her and give her a hard time about her body. Just the other day, a boy passed her in the hall and snickered, "It's going to take a lot more than a few paperback books to hide those jugs." He then proceeded to knock Brenda's books onto the floor. The other students in the hallway chuckled aloud, but Brenda held her head down in shame. The girls in her class always exclude Brenda from their social events. They call her 3-B: "Big Boobed Bimbo." Brenda tried confronting the girls who were teasing her: "I can't help it if I look different than you. Can't you understand this? Please stop teasing me." The girls refused to leave her alone. They just continued to mock her. Brenda confided in her sister, who told her to tell the teacher. However, Brenda felt there was no use in doing this since "the teacher already ignores what is going on."

SCENARIO 2

Paulo is a bright student in the seventh grade. He works very hard and has never received less than an A on his report card. Paulo consistently finishes his assignments on time and is always prepared for class. The teachers find him a joy in the classroom and often use him as a role model for their students. Today, like many days in math class, when one student got an answer wrong, the teacher turned to Paulo and said, "Paulo, would you share the correct answer with the rest of the class?" Paulo answered correctly. The teacher praised him, but the other stu-

dents rolled their eyes and whispered snide remarks: "Teacher's pet," "Brown noser," "Dork."

SCENARIO 3

In Jefferson Middle School there is a secret club for girls. The three girls who are in charge of the club are bossy and downright mean. These girls have been spreading vicious rumors and ethnic slurs. They have targeted two students, Lakisha, who is African American, and Holly, who is of Asian descent. Lakisha and Holly frequently visit the nurse's office during their lunch hour with complaints of headaches, nausea, and dizziness. Teachers have never directly witnessed the verbal assaults, but they have received grievances from other students. Lakisha and Holly have been reluctant to report these episodes. Within the past 2 weeks, Lakisha has missed 5 school days. Holly has attended class but often appears distracted.

SCENARIO 4

Since the third grade, Marcus has been teased, pushed, and kicked by the other boys in his class. He used to "suck it up" until he got home from school, where he would cry himself to sleep each night. Now he is in the sixth grade, and the same boys continue to bully him. The only thing that has changed is that Marcus has decided to fight back. He is tired of being threatened at the bus stop, followed home, cornered in the bathroom, and made to eat dirt during P.E. He stole a knife from his father's tool box and is prepared to deal with his enemies. A student who has a locker near Marcus's saw the knife and reported it to the principal.

SCENARIO 5

Ms. M., a seventh-grade teacher, overhears Johnny, Alan, and Sam discussing a situation in which a classmate is being bullied. They express their dismay in seeing this person bullied but are unsure about what they should do. Johnny thinks that if they intervene they will make it worse and may cause the bully to turn on them. Alan thinks that they should stand up for the bullied person the next time it happens. Sam just doesn't know which idea is best.

When reading these situations, did you think about a student or students you once had or now have in your class? Perhaps one of the situations even reminded you of an event you were involved in as a child. Teachers frequently ask the following questions about these scenarios. Please pause to answer each question before reading the answer that follows.

Question: In which of these situations does bullying take place?

Answer: Bullying behaviors are exhibited in all of the scenarios. Each meets the Double I/R criteria. Scenario 5 represents an example of bystanders' failing to offer help to someone being victimized. In cases like this, both the bystanders and the bully's target are victimized. Bystanders fail to respond because, among other reasons, they are insensitive to the distress the bullying is causing, they fear they will become the bully's next target, or they are uncertain whom to turn to because their past attempts to solicit help from adults have been unsuccessful.

Question: How do the bullying behaviors in these situations vary?

Answer: The bullying behaviors involve both physical and psychological intimidation and abuse, including behaviors such as sexual harassment, teasing, verbal threats, pushing, and kicking. Scenario 3 illustrates warning signals, or "secondary signs" of victimization: physical symptoms, frequent visits to the school nurse, increased absenteeism, and lack of participation. Victimization is sometimes overlooked or disregarded when only secondary signs are present.

Question: How do the boys' and girls' bullying behaviors differ?

Answer: The situations illustrate bullying incidents involving both males and females. In general, boys tend to engage in physical means of bullying—what is called *direct bullying*—whereas girls tend to engage in *indirect* or *relational bullying* (e.g., exclusion or spreading rumors). With this in mind, return to Scenarios 3 and 4. Is the difference between indirect and direct bullying apparent? It is important to point out that girls also are quite capable of engaging in direct forms of bullying, and boys frequently engage in name-calling and "dissing" that goes well beyond playful teasing. In all cases, verbal abuse can escalate into physical aggression, commonly as the bully becomes more and more provocative or the victim reaches a breaking point and strikes back in frustration.

Question: How do these incidents of bullying differ from typical childhood rough-and-tumble play?

Answer: The main difference between the bullying behaviors represented in the scenarios and typical childhood play is that the physical and psychological harm inflicted is intentional. For instance, in Scenario 1, the teasing of Brenda by her classmates is not done in a friendly way, but is motivated by the intent to hurt her.

To help you determine whether behaviors you have witnessed in and around your classroom constitute bullying, think of several incidents in the last month in which one or more students appeared to be abusive or aggressive toward another student. Now apply the Double I/R criteria:

- Was the behavior committed *intentionally* to inflict harm on another?

- Was there an *imbalance* of power between the two students, such that one could be defined as a bully and the other a victim?

- Was the behavior inflicted *repeatedly?* That is, did it happen more than once, and was there a pattern to the occurrence?

A PERSONAL DEFINITION OF BULLYING

Now take a moment to jot down your own working definition of bullying. Does your definition include the concepts of intention, imbalance, and repetition? Go back to the "expert" definitions presented earlier and reread them. How do they compare with your own definition of bullying? If needed, take a minute to revise your definition. Make sure your definition is "user friendly"—that it defines bullying in your own words and makes sense to you. Turn to the Personal Goals Form on page 34. On a photocopy of the form, write your definition in the space indicated, where you can refer to it at any time.

ROLE OF TEACHERS

If someone is pushing you around there is no one to tell. . . . You have to take care of it yourself. . . . If you run and tell the teachers they think you are a punk. When they think you're a punk, you know you've got to watch your back.

—13-year-old boy

If you are aware that bullying exists, what can you do? Many teachers are unsure what their role is in addressing bullying problems. If they perceive bullying as "child's play" or fear that intervening will only make the victim's situation worse, they are unlikely to feel it is right to intervene. However, both victims and bullies need their teachers' help. Youth depend on adults when they are unable to solve problems on their own. This is particularly true in the bullying interaction, where there are serious and long-lasting consequences for all parties involved.

You have the ability to heighten your awareness of what maintains bullying interactions in your classroom, and you have the ability to change the situation. Certain teacher beliefs and actions maintain bullying; others serve to prevent or reduce it.

Teacher Beliefs and Actions That Maintain Bullying

- Believing they shouldn't intervene in bullying because they lack adequate skills and training (Stephenson & Smith, 1989)

- Fearing that intervening will only "add fuel to the fire" and result in increased bullying of some children (Besag, 1989)

- Ignoring bullying incidents, therefore perpetuating students' belief that teachers are unaware of the problem (Bryne, 1994a, 1994b)

- Failing to intervene at all or doing so only "once in a while"

Teacher Beliefs and Actions That Prevent or Reduce Bullying

- Increasing their knowledge and skills by reading the material in this manual and other sources, and by putting what they learn into practice. (The more you practice, the more you will believe in your ability to utilize the skills you have acquired.)

- Recognizing that they cannot effectively intervene, removing themselves from the situation long enough to review it, and consulting with other members of the Support Team. If necessary, teachers can help students find assistance elsewhere (e.g., from the school counselor, principal, another teacher).

- Letting students know they are aware of bullying incidents by introducing the topic of bullying into the classroom curriculum and by integrating activities like the ones described in this manual to increase students' awareness and understanding of the bullying problem

- Working to identify and intervene in every instance of bullying

- Establishing an "open door" policy to encourage students to feel free to speak to those in authority

CORE CONDITIONS FOR PREVENTING AND REDUCING BULLYING

Children look to teachers for support and encouragement, and teachers have the power to make significant differences in children's lives. In order for efforts to intervene in bullying to succeed, teachers need to establish certain core conditions. Specifically, you will need to do as follows:

- Become aware of the bully/victim problems in your classroom and school. The information in this module has helped you begin that process.

- Serve as a model for students. You have an innate power to set precedents and guide behaviors in your classroom.

- Serve as a change agent. Monitoring and altering your own behavior can facilitate changes in your students' behavior. Monitoring your students' behavior will help you become more aware of bullying incidents, thus allowing you to intervene and facilitate change.

- Recognize and identify differing forms of bullying and victimization.

- Be able to identify differences between male and female bullies.

- Learn skills necessary for intervening in bullying situations.

- Learn skills necessary for assisting victims.

- Learn prevention strategies specifically related to the problem of bullying and victimization.

- Integrate prevention activities into the curriculum.

- Believe that you can obtain the knowledge and skills to intervene and prevent classroom bullying.

- Believe in your ability to make a difference in your students.

- Use this manual and other resources to help prevent and reduce bullying (attend bullying prevention workshops and seminars, join teacher support groups, participate in group problem solving, and consult with school counselors, school psychologists, or other teachers for advice).

Subsequent modules will give you the information you need to establish these core conditions.

CONTENT REVIEW

The following statements refer to the learning goals of this module. Take a minute to think about the statements. Ask yourself whether you feel confident that you can say yes to each. If not, take some time to revisit those topics and consider ways to strengthen your learning.

I am more aware of the extent and seriousness of the bullying problem.	Yes ❑	No ❑
I can recognize the Double I/R criteria for bullying as inflicting *intentional* harm, occurring in a relationship characterized by *imbalance* of power, and taking place *repeatedly* over time.	Yes ❑	No ❑
I am able to apply the Double I/R criteria to situations occurring in my own school.	Yes ❑	No ❑
I have developed a personal working definition of bullying.	Yes ❑	No ❑
I am aware of my role as a change agent to prevent and intervene in bullying situations.	Yes ❑	No ❑
I have established/am working to establish the core conditions for preventing and reducing bullying.	Yes ❑	No ❑

A Reminder . . .

CLASSROOM INTERACTION AND AWARENESS CHART

Use the CIAC to describe any bullying behavior you observe (and that students report to you, if you wish). Specific instructions for filling out the CIAC appear in Appendix D, along with a blank copy of the chart.

THE BIG QUESTIONS

Focus yourself and honestly appraise your progress by asking yourself the "Big Questions." There are no right or wrong answers.

In relation to bullying in my school:

1. What is my goal?

2. What am I doing?

3. Is what I am doing helping me achieve my goal?

4. *(If not)* What can I do differently?

PERSONAL GOALS FORM

The Personal Goals Form, on the next page, is designed to help you tailor the content of this module to your own students and situation. If you have not filled out the form as you worked through the information component of the module, please take a moment to do so now.

Personal Goals Form

GOALS

- To become aware of the scope of the bullying problem

- To understand and apply the "Double I/R" criteria for bullying

- To develop a personal definition of bullying

- To identify teachers' role in the prevention and remediation of bullying

- To learn the core conditions for reducing bullying and victimization

1. My personal definition of bullying:

   _____

   _____

   _____

2. I have observed incidents of bullying in my classroom. *(Please record incidents on the Classroom Interaction and Awareness Chart.)*

3. I will conduct the following classroom activities to help my students become more aware of bullying:

   _____

   _____

4. I will evaluate the effectiveness of these activities by (a) recording incidents on the CIAC to see if there is a reduction across time, (b) monitoring the extent to which students report bullying situations, and (c) recording my impressions of change in the classroom environment. *(Please indicate any other means of evaluation in the space below.)*

   _____

   _____

5. I will give students feedback by (a) sharing the number and types of incidents recorded on the CIAC and (b) encouraging classroom discussion of these incidents and related issues. *(Please indicate any other means of giving feedback in the space below.)*

   _____

   _____

6. I will share my experiences in applying the information in this module with members of my Support Team, other teachers, administrators, parents. *(Please specify who and when in the space below.)*

   _____

   _____

Classroom Activities

WALKING THE BEAT

This activity is used to heighten students' awareness of bullying as well as to provide you with information concerning when and where bullying in your school is occurring. Students become detectives in investigating "cases" of bullying. Each day, you can check in with the "investigators" and discuss any bullying that is occurring.

FRAMING THE BULLY

Almost every student has had a very personal experience with a bully. This exercise provides an opportunity for students to express what they believe a bully is and does. Together, the class can create their own definition of bullying and brainstorm ways in which they can help intervene in and prevent bullying.

STOP, REWIND, PLAY IT AGAIN

Often students and adults say things to others in an inappropriate and hurtful manner without even acknowledging their own behavior. This activity helps students become more aware of what they say to others and practice more constructive means of expressing themselves.

Walking the Beat

OBJECTIVES

- To help students become aware of bullying that is occurring in school
- To encourage students to take an active role in identifying such problems

MATERIALS

- Officer's Report Form
- Chalkboard or easel pad

DIRECTIONS

1. Discuss with students the importance of becoming aware of bullying in the school. Provide examples of bullying behaviors—for example, teasing, pushing, making fun, and so forth.

2. Give each student a copy of the Officer's Report Form and let students know you will make extra copies of the form available in the classroom in a central location. Explain that students may pick up a form each time they witness a bullying incident and that they may record as many bullying incidents as they wish.

3. They will record the following information about bullying incidents: date/time of the incident, location of the incident, and a brief description of the event. On the chalkboard or easel pad, write the following example. Discuss any questions.

    Officer on duty: Beth S.

    Date/time of report: April 9, 12:30 P.M.

    Location: Girls' bathroom

    Description of event: Three girls were in the bathroom. Two of the girls were making fun of the other girl by saying she was fat.

4. Assure the students that because this is an educational experience, they can talk to you about their observations openly, without feeling they are "tattling" on classmates. Students may feel more comfort-

able not disclosing names. Let students know that signing their names to the forms is optional, but that if they want or need follow through from you, the school counselor, or an administrator, you will need to have their names. Just as police officers sign their reports, students who expect to reduce bullying will need to let you know who is making the report.

5. Close the activity by asking the discussion questions. Each day, take a few minutes to check in with the class to allow them to discuss what they have observed. Remind students that they can ask you questions privately at any time.

DISCUSSION

- Where does bullying occur?

- Does everyone bully?

- Are there certain types of students who bully more than others?

- Has someone bullied you? How did it feel?

- Do other people help out when someone is being bullied? Why or why not?

NOTE

This exercise requires a delicate balance between developing students' understanding of bullying and maintaining students' rights to privacy and confidentiality. Depending on the students in your class, you may want to consider the following options:

- If students are able to keep their materials to themselves, have them keep the reports in their notebooks, then bring them to class for discussion.

- If students are unorganized and unlikely to keep their materials together, provide copies of the report form at the beginning of class. At the end of class, have students drop off any filled-out forms at your desk or in a box.

- Rather than have students select which events to discuss in class, review the report forms first and select specific events you believe analyzing will help students develop a better understanding of bullying. You may want to review these events with your Support Team and practice your presentation with them before working with the students directly.

OFFICER'S REPORT FORM

INCIDENT REPORT

Officer on duty: _____

Date/time of report: _____

Location: _____

Description of event: _____

_____

_____

_____

_____

INCIDENT REPORT

Officer on duty: _____

Date/time of report: _____

Location: _____

Description of event: _____

_____

_____

_____

_____

INCIDENT REPORT

Officer on duty: _____

Date/time of report: _____

Location: _____

Description of event: _____

_____

_____

_____

_____

Framing the Bully

OBJECTIVES

- To increase students' awareness, understanding, and identification of bullying behaviors and characteristics
- To create a definition of bullying in order to assist students in openly discussing the problem of bullying within the classroom
- To assist students in identifying their role in bully prevention

MATERIALS

- Framing the Bully handout
- Art supplies (crayons, markers, colored pencils)
- Chalkboard or easel pad

DIRECTIONS

1. Distribute art supplies and copies of the Framing the Bully handout.

2. Ask the students to define *bullying* by drawing pictures, using symbols, and writing a few words inside the picture frame. (Note: Students' names should not be written.)

3. On the chalkboard or easel pad, write, "What is a bully?" Have the students discuss their pictures and the words they used to describe bullying. Record their descriptions as they volunteer them.

4. Have the students add more words to their pictures that they feel apply to bullying. They can keep this sheet to refer to when they question whether or not a particular behavior is bullying. They also can continue to add words as they gain increased awareness of bullying behaviors.

5. Process the activity by discussing the following questions.

DISCUSSION

- How do you react when you encounter a person who has the characteristics we have listed?

- How do you think the bully sees these characteristics in himself or herself?

- How do you think the bully comes to have these characteristics?

- Is someone who bullies always a bully in all situations? What are some examples?

- If there is a difference between how you see the bully and how the bully sees himself or herself, why do you suppose that is?

- How might we redefine these characteristics as positives or help a bully use these characteristics in a positive way? (For instance, we could help the bully use strength to become a good leader instead of picking on others.)

NOTE

This is a very powerful activity. If there are bullies in the class, they may be hearing for the first time how their classmates view them. It is therefore important to stress that bullying behaviors are learned (perhaps in response to a difficult environment), that students who bully at school may not bully in other situations (e.g., home, church, sports), and that bullying characteristics can be looked at in a positive way.

FRAMING THE BULLY

Stop, Rewind, Play It Again

OBJECTIVES

- To bring attention to bullying behaviors

- To help classroom bullies recognize their behaviors and how they are affecting others

- To help all students learn new, more appropriate ways to interact with others

MATERIALS

- Stop, Rewind, Play It Again worksheet

DIRECTIONS

1. Emphasize to the class that there will always be someone we may not get along with (e.g., a peer, sibling, teacher, and so forth) and that if we don't take that person's feelings into consideration, we may say or do something that is hurtful to the person.

2. Explain that this activity will help the group become aware of how they are treating others and how others are treating them. Tell students that when one student makes a negative comment toward another student, teacher, or other person, you will ask that student to restate the comment in a more positive way. For example, if someone calls another class member a "nerd" because she received the highest grade on a test, you will identify that behavior as unacceptable. At that time, you will ask the student who called the other person a nerd to restate the comment—for example, "You work hard and deserve good grades." The reframed comment requires that the opinion be stated in a constructive manner.

3. Distribute copies of the Stop, Rewind, Play It Again worksheet. Pair class members and ask them to practice reframing negative comments as constructive, positive statements. The pairs may work together to generate their own negative comment and restated positive response.

4. After the pairs have had a chance to work through the items, reassemble the class and process the activity by discussing the following questions.

DISCUSSION

1. What are some examples of negative statements students make?

2. Why do you think some students say these things?

3. How do you think the students to whom these statements are directed feel when they hear these things?

4. What are some alternative things that could be said?

5. What can be done to increase the likelihood that these kinder alternative statements will be used?

6. What might be appropriate to do if you have nothing positive to say?

NOTE

The procedure explained in this activity should be used in the classroom periodically to help students reframe negative statements. Encourage students to listen for negative comments and to help one another find ways to restate them in a more positive manner. You can also point out that if students really have nothing positive to say, it is appropriate to elect silence (e.g., not commenting at all if you really don't like another person's clothing) or to make neutral statements (e.g., "I see you have a new haircut").

STOP, REWIND, PLAY IT AGAIN

INSTRUCTIONS

For each negative comment listed below, write a more appropriate or constructive comment.

NEGATIVE COMMENT	POSITIVE ALTERNATIVE
1 You are an airhead.	**1** _____
2 You always brown-nose the teacher.	**2** _____
3 You are a nerd.	**3** _____
4 I can't stand you.	**4** _____
5 Your clothes are ugly.	**5** _____

INSTRUCTIONS

What mean or negative thing have you said to someone or has someone said to you? Write it down in the following space and then restate it in a positive way.

NEGATIVE COMMENT	POSITIVE ALTERNATIVE
_____	_____
_____	_____
_____	_____
_____	_____
_____	_____
_____	_____

MODULE

2 Recognizing the Bully

OVERVIEW

Take a moment and close your eyes. With your eyes closed, remember when you were in school, when you were the age of the students you are now teaching. Was there a bully? Picture that person. Does a specific image come to mind? Now shift your perspective to your own teaching situation and think of a bully. Are you envisioning a student you know, one who is part of a problem in your teaching today? Each of us holds a specific idea of what constitutes a bully. If you ask a group of teachers to describe a bully, they will likely describe the stereotype: big, mean, impatient, aggressive, and less intelligent than most other children. There are, however, different kinds of bullies and different forms of bullying. Before implementing any plans for change, we will need to recognize who the bullies are and how children develop into bullies. With knowledge of the social and environmental factors influencing bullying behavior, we can work to change bullies' behavior and to reduce victimization.

GOALS

- To understand theories of how bullying behavior develops

- To recognize aggressive and passive forms of bullying

- To identify differences between male and female bullying

- To challenge myths and misconceptions related to bullying

DEVELOPMENT OF BULLYING BEHAVIORS

Bullies are the boys who think they can beat you at anything . . . basketball, grades. . . . They think they can do anything better than you. . . . They're so competitive.

—13-year-old boy

As we witness the harm committed by bullies, it is easy to overlook that these children have needs as well. Bullies are frequently misunderstood. Often, the bully is a victim in other settings, perhaps the target of abuse from family members and/or peers. Understanding how bullying behaviors develop makes it possible for us to expand our responses beyond punishment to include healing and rehabilitation. In the following pages, we first give some background for understanding the development of bullying. We then describe two systems models: the concentric circle model and our own bully-development model.

Background

Studies of the impact of temperament on future behavior show that some children are more active at birth, have more problems relating to others, and are more difficult for parents and teachers to manage (Forehand & Long, 1996; Horne & Sayger, 2000; Martin, 1988). These biological tendencies have an effect on whether or not a child becomes a bully; however, social interactions are more powerful influences.

The *social-interactional model of aggression* seems particularly appropriate for developing an understanding of both bullying and victim behaviors, especially in school settings. Social learning theory asserts that children learn to behave as they do through their experiences in social settings (Bandura, 1973). All children behave egocentrically when they are very young, as though they are the center of the universe, but most children learn over time to be more reciprocal in their relationships, to give and take, to share and be shared with. This learning occurs in the social settings of the family and the community. Even children who are temperamentally more active and at times more difficult to be with can learn to be socially appropriate and respectful of others. In other words, biological tendencies are affected by the social environment.

If the social setting emphasizes working together, cooperation, and effective problem solving, children will learn nonaggressive ways to handle the stress and conflict they will invariably encounter with other children. When the social environment teaches children to manage conflict through aggression and coercion, they learn that problems are best solved through the use of power. They begin to respond as though others in the world are "out to get them." These children lack trust, do not develop respect or appreciation for others, and do not see cooperation and collaboration as means to accomplish their goals.

The interactional aspect of learning suggests that all people interact in their social environments and that they are influenced by others. People also influence the world of which they are a part—in other words, in a social interaction, all parts influence all other parts. Thus, bullies in the classroom influence the other members of the class, but members of the class—and particularly the teacher—also influence bullies.

Basically, then, bullying behavior is learned in a social situation and is influenced and maintained in interactions with others. Social learning–interactional theory is based on the assumption of "triadic reciprocal causality," a fancy way of saying that an individual creates and alters the *environment*, the environment shapes his or her *behavior*, and the individual's *cognitions* are the mediators of his or her behavior (Bandura, 1977, 1986).

Learning

Bullying behaviors are learned, either directly or vicariously. *Direct learning* is learning experienced directly, specifically by doing. For example, if one child pushes another child off a swing, then gets to use the swing sooner, the first child learns directly that force (in this case, pushing) leads to getting what he or she wants. *Vicarious learning* is learning experienced indirectly, specifically by observing another's actions and the consequences of those actions. If a third child on the playground witnesses the first child's successful takeover of the swing by pushing, that child may learn vicariously that force is an effective way to get what one wants. This type of learning occurs when children observe successful acts of aggression in real life, as well as in movies, television, song lyrics, and so forth. In addition, parents or other care-takers who model aggressive behaviors are often sources of vicarious learning. One of our clients (his name has been changed) expressed the dynamics of family modeling as follows:

> Raymond was incarcerated at the Youth Detention Center, where his good sense of humor and talkativeness made him popular with others at the institution, including fellow incarcerated youth and the officers. He bragged, "Everyone in my family loves to fight. That's why I'm in here. I love to fight." (Horne, Glaser, & Sager, 1994, p. 2)

Consequences

A person's perceptions of the consequences (positive reinforcement, negative reinforcement, or punishment) of a behavior determine whether or not the behavior will be maintained. *Positive reinforcement* increases the frequency of a behavior. When bullies get their way, they are being positively reinforced and are more likely to continue to engage in the same behavior. The reinforcement may be direct (getting to use the swing more) or it may be cognitive (getting pleasure out of being bigger than someone else and being able to make that person do as one demands).

Negative reinforcement increases the frequency of a behavior by removing an aversive, or unpleasant, stimulus. If peers who previously have condemned bullying behavior begin to ignore such situations, the bullying behavior will increase.

Punishment decreases the frequency of a behavior. For instance, when bullies receive consequences they do not like—being placed in time-out or being removed from the classroom—this is punishment. The difficulty is making sure the response actually is punishing to the individual. Bullies often look upon consequences that would appear punishing as desirable. For example, being removed from the classroom and sent to the principal's office may promote a "tough-guy image." If the behavior is decreasing, the punishment is working. If the behavior is not decreasing, the consequence is not punishment.

Behavior

Bullying behaviors can take a number of different forms, among them the following:

- Verbal threats, harassment, intimidation

- Teasing, taunting, annoying

- Spreading rumors

- Striking, slapping

- Pushing, shoving

- Instigating fights

Cognitive Factors

Cognitions, or thoughts or perceptions about an event, are different in children who bully and those who do not. Often, bullies misperceive cues in the environment and make erroneous assumptions about what is going on. For example, if one child pats a child prone to bullying on the back in a friendly way, the second child may perceive the touch as an act of aggression or threat. The bully may see an accidental bump as a push or shove, then retaliate. The bully also is likely to perceive the rewards of his or her behavior as outweighing the costs and the victim's distress as positive reinforcement, thus perpetuating the bully/victim cycle.

One of the most difficult aspects of working with bullies is figuring out their cognitive processes—how they think—and then working to change those cognitions. Most children develop empathic ability naturally. Unfortunately, a minority of children find it difficult to care about and understand the emotions of others. We believe this deficit is a function of these children's belief that they have not been understood or treated fairly and their consequent desire or need to treat others as they believe they have been treated. If children think they have been wronged, they will behave as though it is true. It is difficult to change this pattern of thinking, but it is important to try to help children learn to challenge the accuracy of their assumptions.

Environmental Factors

Three environments are influential in determining whether or not a child becomes a bully: the family, the school, and the community.

Family environment

Often, bullies come from families characterized by poverty, conflict, inconsistent parenting, and/or harsh discipline. Parents may contribute to the development of bullying by modeling aggression, setting inadequate limits, providing inconsistent supervision, and implementing inappropriate punishments.

We have worked extensively with families who have aggressive children and have published the results of this work in *Troubled Families* (Fleischman, Horne, & Arthur, 1982) and *Treating Conduct and Oppositional Defiant Disorders in Children* (Horne & Sayger, 1990). Representing more than 20 years of study, our findings suggest that the higher the rate of aggression in the family, the higher the rate in the children. However, children's aggressive behavior in the family can be substantially reduced if they are provided with structure in the family, receive clear and concise communication about what is expected of them, and have family members who exercise restraint and control. Families can learn to provide appropriate consequences for children's behavior: reinforcement for appropriate behavior (smiles and touches, point systems, allowances, time with family or friends) and appropriate discipline for aggressive behavior. Both natural consequences (e.g., being hungry if you forget to pack your lunch) and logical consequences (e.g., having friends begin to avoid or confront an aggressor) work to reduce aggression in children.

Two things stand out especially in our research: Children want consistency and predictability in their families, and they want to be treated fairly and with dignity. When these conditions are absent, aggression is frequently the outcome. Inconsistent punishment for aggression does not reduce aggression; it teaches children to figure out when punishment won't happen and to be wiser in their use of aggression, or it results in their feeling they have been treated unjustly. Bullies are often seeking revenge for the injustice in their lives by being unjust to the less powerful in their schools. The following example of Ned and his mother illustrates some of these factors.

> *Ned, a sixth grader, never knew what to expect from his mother. She abused alcohol and sometimes had a job, sometimes not. Ned could never guess what her mood would be when he got home from school. Sometimes she had had a few drinks and was funny, and they laughed together a lot. Other times she would have had too much to drink and be very irritable. When that happened, she inevitably spanked Ned or punished him in some other physical way. When Ned was spanked, he would get very angry at his mother and everybody else. He generally carried the anger with him to school the next day. He often sought out younger boys on the playground. He pushed and shoved the smaller kids and would demand their lunch money. He knew they had not done anything to him, but he also knew he was mad and someone deserved to be pushed around, so it might as well be the smaller kids at school.*

Ned's bullying behavior is a result of his direct and indirect learning experiences. Although his behavior does not seem logical or rational to most, his irrational thoughts that the younger kids "deserve it" and his maladaptive behaviors in response to those thoughts keep him in trouble.

School environment

A number of factors in the school environment can contribute to the development and maintenance of bullying behavior, among them the following:

- School discipline (either too authoritarian or too lax)

- Reinforcement, many times unintentional, of bullying behavior by school personnel (also ignoring of bullying incidents)

- Peer groups with a norm of aggressive behavior

- Modeling by school staff and other students of aggressive or coercive behaviors

Community environment

As we said earlier, one way children learn to be aggressive is by observing aggressive behaviors in others. Individuals reared in a nonaggressive culture will themselves learn nonaggressive behaviors by watching and interacting with the models in their lives. Children raised in a culture marked by conflict and violent interactions will learn aggressive responses. Often, bullying behaviors are modeled and reinforced by neighbors and other community members. Children may be told to "Stand up for yourself" or "Fight like a man." When children live in a community in which aggression and coercion are successful, they learn to get what they want by becoming even more aggressive.

In one of our recent surveys, we learned that the majority of children involved in bullying incidents in elementay school had been told by family members to use force and fight if necessary to get others to do what they wanted. Even telling children to take care of themselves by fighting in self-defense leads to increased aggression in schools.

Bullying starts in neighborhoods and families. . . . Some people grow up in homes where they learn to push others around, so they think it's OK.

—13-year-old boy

Systems Models of Bullying

Bullying does not occur in isolation. It is the result of the interactions among a variety of systems, including the home, school, community, and society at large. Two models that focus on the interrelationships among systems in the development of aggression are the concentric circle model and our own bully-development theory.

The Concentric Circle Model

Fried and Fried (1996) have used the concentric circle model to illustrate how three systems interact in the development of aggression. As shown, the major factors are the child, family, school, community, and culture.

The child

The innermost circle encompasses the child's personality traits (e.g., temperament, self-esteem), physical characteristics (e.g., tall, strong), and behaviors (e.g., aggressive, immature). These qualities influence the child's early family interactions as well as interactions with other children. Children are not seen as being born predisposed to perform specific aggressive acts; rather, the underlying assumption is that aggressive behavior is learned.

The family

The bully at school is often the victim at home and has caretakers who use physical means of discipline, provide little supervision, are hostile, rejecting, authoritarian, inconsistent in their parenting, lack effective

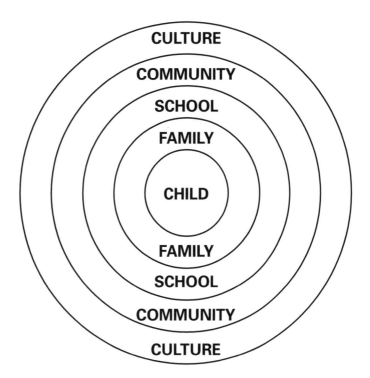

problem-solving skills, and teach their children to strike back when provoked (Batsche & Knoff, 1994; Fleischman et al., 1982; Floyd, 1985; Horne & Sayger, 1990; Patterson, 1982). Aggressive children have family members who tend to use ineffective discipline practices, which include coercion, inconsistency, and harsh punishment (Olweus, 1978; Patterson, 1986). Caretakers provide inadequate emotional support and are likely to display a lack of warmth or caring toward their children. In addition, marital conflict, single-parent households, and low income may all contribute to the development of bullying behavior (Horne & Sayger, 1990; Stephenson & Smith, 1987).

The school

Aggression and bullying behavior are traditions in American schools, and these beliefs seem to be deeply embedded in the schools' culture (Wilezenski et al., 1994; Young, 1994). In schools, bullying is often legitimized. This perception is fostered by the disciplinary philosophy of the school as well as the teachers', administrators', and counselors' competence and willingness to intervene in student conflicts. Nonintervention by school personnel may be perceived as approval of the aggressor, thereby reinforcing aggression (Fried & Fried, 1996; Hoover et al., 1992).

The community

The neighborhood in which one resides, the economic level of the community, and the ethnic diversification of the community all influence the development of bullying behaviors. In addition, the attitude of the community can have a significant effect on the interpersonal relationships considered acceptable (Fried & Fried, 1996). Sanctioning or tolerating bullying may be the result of the community's inability and lack of interest in supporting any antibullying solutions (Young, 1994).

The culture

The cultural context exerts a tremendous influence on the development and maintenance of bullying behavior. The cultural context sanctions and reinforces tolerance of bullying, a fact underscored by the role of the media in shaping the values of the American culture (e.g., in television programs, bullying is often disregarded or approved; Fried & Fried, 1996; Horne et al., 1994). In addition, there is a general consensus that active and assertive behavior is a normal and desirable characteristic for American children (Olweus, 1994).

The Bully-Development Model

Another way of looking at the influences of the child, family, neighborhood, school, and community is provided in our own model of bully development, diagrammed on the next page. The *culture* is a contextual variable that umbrellas the entire model. In brief, culture encompasses societal norms, which are highly influential in bullying. The society at large has a profound influence in determining what is acceptable within that culture. In simplified terms, the predominant culture impacts the *community,* affecting *family demographics. Disrupted family management* may result in *weak conventional bonding* with the child, associated with *hostile parent/child interaction* and an *inconsistent parenting* style. These interaction styles may influence how the child's *temperament* is manifested in behavior, which in turn influences that child's *cognitive ability* to interpret environmental cues. For example, the child might misinterpret a pat on the back as a push or shove, an act of aggression or a threat. This potentially leads to *bullying behaviors* inside and outside of the school. The bullying behaviors are often positively *reinforced by peers*: Spectators may express interest and admiration for the manipulations of the bully. In addition, it is not uncommon for bullying to be *ignored or sanctioned by teachers* who mistakenly believe that the children involved will "work it out on their own." Imagine as an adult becoming involved in a conflict with a much larger person on a downtown street in your town or city. Imagine further that a police officer comes to the scene and says, "You look like adults—you two work this out," then walks away, leaving you face to face with this large, menacing person. This is often the situation our children encounter. This general tolerance of bullying then contributes to the societal acceptance of bullying in our *culture.* In this continuous feedback loop, then, bullying behaviors amplify, resulting in more and more school violence.

We have taken the liberty of expanding on several of the model's components in the following discussion.

Cultural factors

The cultural norms—the guidelines of the greater society—impact the community in which people live, with communities reflecting the greater cultural norms. Likewise, community norms influence the lives of families in the neighborhoods, such that the families live consistently with the community expectations for the neighborhood.

THE BULLY-DEVELOPMENT MODEL

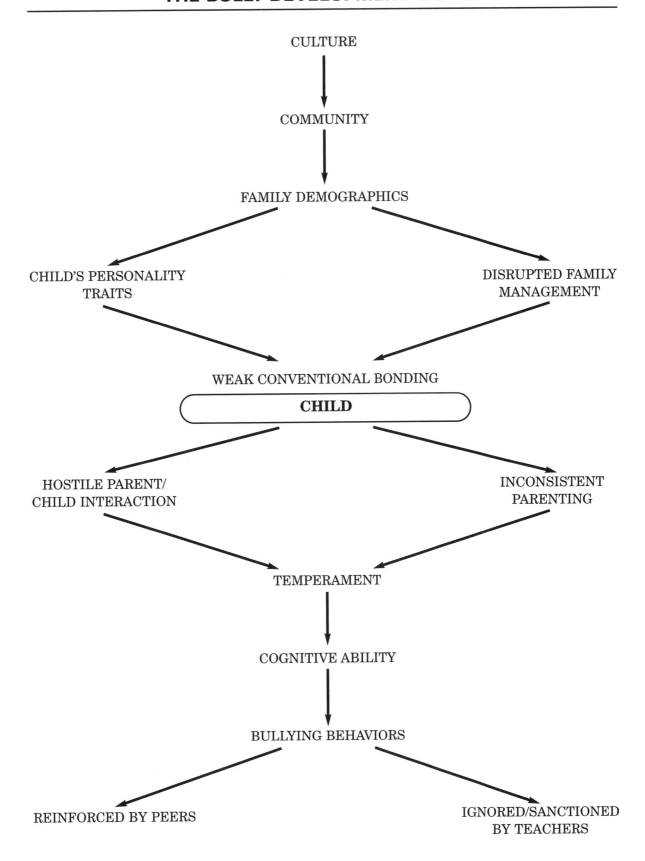

CULTURE

↓

COMMUNITY

↓

FAMILY DEMOGRAPHICS

CHILD'S PERSONALITY TRAITS

DISRUPTED FAMILY MANAGEMENT

WEAK CONVENTIONAL BONDING

CHILD

HOSTILE PARENT/ CHILD INTERACTION

INCONSISTENT PARENTING

TEMPERAMENT

↓

COGNITIVE ABILITY

↓

BULLYING BEHAVIORS

REINFORCED BY PEERS

IGNORED/SANCTIONED BY TEACHERS

Culture is like an umbrella: It reaches over all aspects of people's lives. Within cultures, norms exist determining what is acceptable and nonacceptable behavior in the society. Societal norms exist that embrace violence and aggression and, in fact, some cultural identities are wrapped in a commitment to aggression. Cultural factors influence the development of children. When the larger culture places an emphasis on violence and aggression, children learn that violence is an acceptable and even an appropriate way to manage conflict.

As an aspect of the larger cultural context, the media play an important role in promoting the acceptance of bullies and their aggressive behaviors. Television programs, news, films, popular music, and video games often show aggression in an attractive light. Many video games clearly extol violence. Heroes in action films frequently use aggressive means to accomplish their ends. Even if the ends are positive and the heroes on the side of "good," this sends the message that power and aggression are required to win. Kind and gentle people are often depicted as powerless, subtly underscoring the idea that social problem solving, cooperation, mediation, and conflict management are ineffective.

Not all children who observe violence in films, video games, or other media will engage in violence themselves; many have learned from their families and communities that aggression really hurts people. Other children, however, may not be able to make that distinction and vicariously learn to add aggression, violence, and bullying to their repertoire of responses, particularly if there are no family discussions to help with this issue.

Family factors

A number of family factors influence the development of aggressive behavior in children. The functioning of the parents strongly influences children's development. In families where there is mental illness (e.g., depression, schizophrenia) there is an increased likelihood of child problems. The parental mental illness does not cause problems in children; rather, children fail to receive the level of nurturing and support they need because families who have to focus their energy on the needs of an ill parent often do not have sufficient resources left over to nurture children.

Another family factor that influences child development is being raised in a single-parent family. Being raised in a single-parent family does not in itself doom a child to problems. In fact, one research study (Horne, 1981) suggested that children having the most problems were indeed from single-parent families; however, on the other end of the continuum, the best-functioning children in the study were also from single-parent families. The difference in the two was the level of support and resources available to the single parent. Those who had good resources and support from other family members and friends did fine as single parents. Those whose resources were in short supply had children who experienced greater problems in development.

Other family problems greatly impact the development of children as well. For example, unemployment, substance abuse, and disruptive patterns in family management all make children's developing healthy and prosocial relationship skills more difficult. Likewise, economic level and community factors influence development—for example, children growing up in housing projects are likely to experience more problems developing prosocial skills. This is not necessarily a function of the housing project or of poverty itself, for many who have grown up poor in America manage to lead healthy and productive lives. The developmental problems are more a function of the lack of resources available to the family, resulting in greater deprivation and the need for parents to be working longer hours, thus not being available to the child.

Family bonding

The extent to which a child is accepted into the family and feels supported, understood, and valued determines the extent to which the child treats others similarly. When children feel safe and secure, they bond with members of the family. This results in a child who is confident, secure, and treats others with respect and dignity, for that is how he or she has been treated within the family structure. When this bonding does not occur, children fail to develop an ability to take the perspective of others: They can't understand the world as others see it. Instead, others are seen as objects, not as people, and objects can be treated with disdain and reacted to aggressively. This situation promotes the making of the bully.

Parent/child interactions

The family has considerable influence on the child. If the family influences are positive, the outcome will be a child with good problem-solving skills who develops appropriate social skills. On the other hand, a child who experiences hostile interactions within the family may become coercive, aggressive, and a bully.

Individual child characteristics

Children are born with certain characteristics that are based on biological influences. Some of the characteristics are fixed at birth—eye and skin color, for example. Other characteristics are affected by interaction with cultural and social influences—intelligence and temperament, for example. While some of these characteristics may lead to troublesome behavior (e.g., being more active and "fussy" as an infant), this is not inevitable. Family and community influences can have a significant impact on whether and how these characteristics are manifested. In a family represented by coercion, aggression, and inconsistent parenting, for example, a child with a predisposition toward being fussy may develop into an aggressive bully. The same child in a family that has consistent routines, provides a lot of support and encouragement, and models effective problem solving will have a very different outcome.

Acceptance/rejection by peers

If a child grows up in a family that is supportive and encouraging, and the child develops appropriate social skills and is able to interact effectively with other children, then the future is positive. The child has the prosocial skills to be accepted by and involved with a supportive peer group. On the other hand, if the child fails to develop appropriate social skills, and in fact resorts to aggression and coercion to have relationships with others, the child will be rejected. When the child is rejected by the peer cohort, he or she resorts to socializing with people who are available: Kids lacking in social skills hang out with other kids who have been rejected by the group, resulting in a delinquent peer group. This group is likely to engage in aggression, bullying, and other forms of antisocial behavior.

The bully's word is law, which reinforces a feeling of power. Bullying allows children who are either bored with school or not doing well to be "good" at something, prove their courage and dominance to their peers. It allows them to feel superior (Ross, 1996). In addition, it eliminates the need for friendship with other children.

It is clear that many factors go into the making of bullies. While we may condemn their behavior, we feel for their plight because they are victims themselves, experiencing pain in trying to find their way. We can be encouraging and supportive, attempting to remediate and rehabilitate rather than condemn and punish. While we approach bullies with a sense of sadness and concern, at the same time we recognize that the bullying must cease. We also accept that our influence is limited over the family and environmental factors that created the bullying condition. We can, however, work with the understanding that children can learn to behave appropriately in the school setting, even if the family or neighborhood situation is less supportive.

DIFFERENT FORMS OF BULLYING

Bullying takes one of two forms: aggressive or passive. Each form can be quite damaging to the victim.

Aggressive Bullies

Ronny was strutting down the hall when Carl accidentally bumped into him. Ronny retaliated by pushing Carl and knocking his books out of his hands. Ronny said that if Carl ever touched him again, he would beat him so hard he would not be able to bump into him again.

CHARACTERISTICS OF AGGRESSIVE BULLIES

- The most common type of bully

- Initiate aggression toward peers

- Characterized as fearless, coercive, tough, and impulsive

- Strong inclination toward violence, a desire to dominate others, and expression of little empathy toward their victims (Olweus, 1994; Ross, 1996)

- Commit open attacks on their victims ("direct bullying")

- Enjoy being in control and wish to subdue others

- Cognitively distort the meaning of their victim's behavior as well as overreact in ambiguous situations

- See the world with a paranoid's eye (Ross, 1996)

Passive Bullies

Sue was having a birthday party, and the whole class was invited. She personally handed out the invitations to her classmates. When she came to Sheila, she said that fat girls were not welcome at her party. Sue's friends began to giggle and whisper to one another as Sheila sat alone at her desk.

CHARACTERISTICS OF PASSIVE BULLIES

- Less common than the aggressive type

- Tend to be dependent, insecure, and anxious

- Participate in bullying but typically do not initiate the aggression

- Intentionally isolate and exclude others from the group ("indirect bullying")

- May lack strong inhibitors against aggression

- Likely to follow suit if they see the aggressive bully's actions being rewarded

- Often lack a defined social status among their peers

- Eager to affiliate with aggressive, action-oriented bullies

- Referred to as "camp followers" or "hangers-on" (Olweus, 1994; Ross, 1996)

Even though it may not be physical, bullying is occurring when students use verbal means to inflict pain on others. Teasing and name-calling are indeed bullying, and it is important to remain aware of the extent of the problem. Whether the bullying is aggressive or passive, the goals of intervention are to help bullies understand the impact of their actions on others (i.e., feel empathy) and to teach more prosocial ways of behaving.

Quite a few teachers with whom we have worked have never considered the kind of passive behaviors shown in the situation about Sue's birthday party to be bullying. When they recognize it as such, some feel discouraged, as though bullying is on the rise. It is likely instead that these teachers are simply becoming more sensitive to the range of bullying behaviors. This is a good sign: The more sensitive teachers become to the extent and forms of bullying, the more they will be inclined to take action to prevent and reduce the problem.

DIFFERENCES BETWEEN MALE AND FEMALE BULLIES

Both boys and girls engage in bullying, although the interactions can be quite different. Following are some points of difference between male and female bullying.

MALE BULLYING

- Negative behavior labeled as "bullying"

- Often engage in direct forms of bullying

- Frequently use visible forms of bullying: pushing, shoving, threatening, and so forth

- Usually bully both sexes

FEMALE BULLYING

- Bullying behavior classified as "mean"

- Often engage in indirect forms of bullying

- Frequently use less visible forms of bullying: slander, spreading rumors, manipulating friendships, and the like

- Usually bully other girls

As noted, it appears that through socialization, boys' often receive the label of "bully" when they commit offenses toward another child. On the other hand, girls' adverse behavior is more often viewed as "mean." Bullying by girls is more difficult to detect because their methods are more indirect. It is important to note, however, that girls are increasingly engaging in physically aggressive bullying. The bullying may begin as verbal, then escalate into physical aggression.

Additional Facts about Male and Female Bullies

- There is a tendency for boys to be exposed to a greater amount of bullying than girls. This trend is marked, primarily in junior high school (Olweus, 1994).

- Worldwide research on bullying has demonstrated consistently that there is a higher incidence of bullying among boys as compared with girls (Ahmad & Smith, 1994).

- Research demonstrates that in the lower grades, the majority of the bullying is committed by older boys (Olweus, 1993).

- Boys who act as bullies are often found to be the oldest members of their peer group (Olweus, 1993).

- Boys engage in direct bullying four times as often as girls and are victimized twice as often (Olweus, 1993).

MYTHS AND MISCONCEPTIONS ABOUT BULLYING

Despite evidence to the contrary, mistaken beliefs about the development of bullying are not uncommon among teachers and others who work with children. As we discuss the broader realm of bullying, teachers often express surprise. In fact, several common myths about bullying influence teachers' perceptions of whether or not bullying is occurring. Following are some of these myths—and their realities.

Myth: The size of a class or school is significant in predicting the frequency of bullying.

Reality: Bullies appear in classrooms and schools of all sizes. A more important factor than the number of students in the room is how the teacher manages the room. The more organized and structured the classroom, the lower the rate of bullying (though the highly structured classroom can go too far in discipline and regulation, resulting in increased negativity among the class). One factor that appears to predict bullying behavior is the amount of unmonitored student time—the less monitoring by an adult, the higher the rate of bullying.

Myth: The aggressive behavior of bullies results from school-related failures and frustrations.

Reality: It is true that bullies often have school-related failures and frustrations. However, the academic failures usually follow the aggressive behavior, not the other way around. In examining aggressive children, it is often evident that they had behavior problems even before they reached their current grade level. The academic problems are likely caused by the behavioral problems because children who are highly active, antagonistic, and aggressive spend more of their time out of their seats and less time oriented toward school tasks.

Myth: Children who are different (e.g., overweight, wear eyeglasses, speak with a different accent) are significantly more likely to be a bully's prey.

Reality: Bullies tend to have an amazing "homing device" that helps them identify other young people who are powerless or at least less powerful. Sometimes the lower power is exemplified in physical characteristics, such as weight problems. But it is not just the weight that causes a bully to attend to certain overweight people; otherwise, all overweight people would have grown up victimized. The attraction for a bully is the lack of power, an understanding that the victim cannot or will not be defended, either by him- or herself, or by peers.

Myth: Bullying is more likely to occur to and from school than at school.

Reality: Although it is true that bullying often does occur away from the school, especially on the school bus, this situation is less common than bullying within the school setting. A major predictor of bullying is unsupervised, unmonitored time, and many bullies have that even at school. Because of the greater accessibility of victims within the school setting, bullies engage in considerably more aggression at school than in other places.

Myth: Students will outgrow aggressive behavior as they get older.

Reality: There often is a reduction of aggressive behavior, on the average, as students move through their academic experiences. This is in part a developmental factor, with students recognizing that they are being ostracized and criticized by their peers. They realize that behavior that was accepted and at times even considered "cute" when they were younger is now seen as immature and unacceptable. On the other hand, students who are impervious to the socializing effects of other students in the school actually may intensify and expand their bullying. They may begin to hang out with others who also engage in aggression, making bullying a group norm for behavior. Although the number of students engaged in bullying may decline with age, then, the severity of the aggression from the remaining students is often high.

Myth: Because students learn to become bullies at home, nothing can be done in the classroom to counteract the influence of the home environment.

Reality: Although it is true that students learn to become bullies in their homes and neighborhoods, students are situational learners. Even though they may have learned bullying behaviors at home, they are so adaptive that, in school, they can and will learn prosocial behaviors if given the opportunity. Small changes in the classroom situation can influence change in other situations. When students learn the advantages of positive behaviors in school, they may be able to transfer the new prosocial behaviors to their homes.

Myth: If parents would do more with their children (e.g., exercise more discipline, teach social skills), then teachers could do more.

Reality: This is partially true. However, children also may have skill deficits in areas in which parents are unable to help them. A more positive way of looking at the situation is to view the teaching of self-discipline and social skills as on a par with the teaching of subject matter. By teaching both subject matter and interpersonal skills, teachers can be a powerful influence in students' lives.

CONTENT REVIEW

The following statements refer to the learning goals of this module. Take a minute to think about the statements. Ask yourself whether you feel confident that you can say yes to each. If not, take some time to revisit those topics and consider ways to strengthen your learning.

I acknowledge that numerous behavioral, cognitive, and environmental factors interact to influence the development of a bully.　　Yes ❏ No ❏

I understand the power of modeling on youths' learning of prosocial and antisocial behaviors. Parents and other adults, peers, and the media can teach youth to respond to others in an aggressive manner.　　Yes ❏ No ❏

I am able to identify both aggressive and passive bullies. Aggressive bullies typically initiate bullying, whereas passive bullies are more likely to use verbal methods and follow aggressive bullies in their taunting.　　Yes ❏ No ❏

I recognize that bullies also have special needs and often have been the victims of aggression in other environments.　　Yes ❏ No ❏

I know the aggressive bully: He or she tends to be a youth who enjoys control and power, and often has little ability to empathize with victims.　　Yes ❏ No ❏

I know the passive bully: He or she tends to be a youth who is insecure, socially anxious, and may have difficulty with peers. The passive bully often can gain power or popularity by associating with the aggressive bully.　　Yes ❏ No ❏

I acknowledge that there are both male and female bullies and their bullying styles tend to differ. Males tend to be more physically aggressive, whereas females more commonly use verbal and social means of victimization.　　Yes ❏ No ❏

I recognize that both sexes are involved in bullying; however, males tend to be involved more frequently both as perpetrators and victims.　　Yes ❏ No ❏

I realize that females typically bully other females, whereas males tend to bully both males and females.　　Yes ❏ No ❏

A Reminder . . .

CLASSROOM INTERACTION AND AWARENESS CHART

Use the CIAC to describe any bullying behavior that you observe (and that students report to you, if you wish). Specific instructions for filling out the CIAC appear in Appendix D, along with a blank copy of the chart.

THE BIG QUESTIONS

Focus yourself and honestly appraise your progress by asking yourself the "Big Questions." There are no right or wrong answers.
In relation to bullying in my school:

1. What is my goal?

2. What am I doing?

3. Is what I am doing helping me achieve my goal?

4. *(If not)* What can I do differently?

PERSONAL GOALS FORM

The Personal Goals Form, on the next page, is designed to help you tailor the content of this module to your own students and situation. If you have not filled out the form as you worked through the information component of the module, please take a moment to do so now.

Personal Goals Form

GOALS

- To understand theories of how bullying develops

- To recognize aggressive and passive forms of bullying

- To identify differences between male and female bullying

- To challenge myths and misconceptions related to bullying

1. My personal perceptions of a bully:

   _____

   _____

2. I have observed incidents of passive and aggressive bullying in my classroom. *(Please record incidents on the Classroom Interaction and Awareness Chart. Specify under "Behaviors" whether incidents are passive or aggressive.)*

3. I will conduct the following classroom activities to help my students become more able to recognize bullies:

   _____

   _____

4. I will evaluate the effectiveness of these activities by (a) recording incidents on the CIAC to see if there is a reduction across time, (b) monitoring the extent to which students report bullying situations, and (c) recording my impressions of change in the classroom environment. *(Please indicate any other means of evaluation in the space below.)*

   _____

   _____

5. I will give students feedback by (a) sharing the number and types of incidents recorded on the CIAC and (b) encouraging classroom discussion of these incidents and related issues. *(Please indicate any other means of giving feedback in the space below.)*

   _____

   _____

6. I will share my experiences in applying the information in this module with members of my Support Team, other teachers, administrators, parents. *(Please specify who and when in the space below.)*

   _____

   _____

Classroom Activities

SHE SAID, HE SAID

This activity is designed to increase students' awareness of differences between boys and girls in terms of bullying behavior. It encourages open discussion of issues related to male and female bullying and allows students to give one another direct feedback.

AN AFTERNOON AT THE MOVIES

It is often easier to discuss issues related to bullying indirectly. Movies offer a safe and fun way to identify different forms of bullying and discuss the consequences of the bully/victim interaction. After watching a movie or scene, students can discuss the interaction among characters and begin to work toward their own solutions to bullying problems.

ON THE OUTSIDE, LOOKING IN

This activity provides students the opportunity to discuss what they think of bullies and how bullies make them feel. Students can express why they believe bullies act in an aggressive manner and what they believe their own role is in combating bullying. (This activity can be reversed to focus on victims.)

She Said, He Said

OBJECTIVES

- To help students become aware of differences between male and female bullies
- For male and female students to share their experiences, opinions, and feelings about bullying incidents

MATERIALS

- She Said, He Said Scenarios

DIRECTIONS

1. Divide the class into two groups: one boys' group and one girls' group.

2. Have the girls' group form a circle, then have the boys' group form another circle, surrounding the girls. (This exercise is often called a "fishbowl" because the outside circle looks into the inside circle.)

3. Select a "She Said" scenario and ask a member of the girls' group to read it aloud. Invite the girls' group to share thoughts and feelings about the incident, why they believe it happened, whether they consider it bullying, and what they could do to prevent or intervene in the situation.

4. After the boys' group has listened to the girls' discussion, invite the boys' group to share thoughts and feelings on how they perceived the incident described in the girls' group and how they may have intervened or prevented it.

5. Have the boys and girls change positions (i.e., boys in the inner circle, girls in the outer). Select a "He Said" scenario and ask a member of the boys' group to read it aloud. Encourage the boys' group to discuss.

6. Alternate discussion of "She Said" and "He Said" scenarios as time permits.

7. Discuss the activity in the larger group, using the following questions.

DISCUSSION

- How did the boys and girls in the scenarios bully in different ways?

- Do boys and girls cope with bullying differently? If so, what are the differences?

- Is there a difference between how boys and girls bully in our school? If so, what?

- Do girls and boys get bullied for different reasons? If so, what are they?

- How would it feel to help someone of the other sex in a bullying situation?

SHE SAID, HE SAID SCENARIOS

SHE SAID

Brenda is a sixth grader whose body is maturing much faster than that of other girls her age. She is embarrassed about her development and often walks down the hall with her books covering her chest. Brenda's classmates, along with other students at school, poke fun at her and give her a hard time about her body. Just the other day, a boy passed her in the hall and snickered, "It's going to take a lot more than a few paperback books to hide those jugs." He then proceeded to knock Brenda's books onto the floor. The other students in the hallway chuckled aloud, but Brenda held her head down in shame. The girls in her class always exclude Brenda from their social events. They call her 3-B: "Big-Boobed Bimbo." Brenda tried confronting the girls who were teasing her: "I can't help it if I look different than you. Can't you understand this? Please stop teasing me." The girls refused to leave her alone. They just continued to mock her. Brenda confided in her sister, who told her to tell the teacher. However, Brenda felt there was no use in doing this since "the teacher already ignores what is going on."

HE SAID

Jamal's family had to move from New Jersey to Georgia when he was in the sixth grade. Jamal was small, less developed than most of the boys in his new class, and lacked the physical ability for sports and games. He appeared timid and withdrawn when he entered school. On his first day, Rodney, a brawny, boisterous classmate, began teasing Jamal about the way he talked, making fun of Jamal's accent and calling him a queer. Jamal began to cry, which provoked Rodney to become even more aggressive. Rodney told the other students he was right because queers cry a lot and are sissies. This caused the other students to laugh and tease Jamal. Each day the taunting and teasing increased, and several of the boys began to push, trip, and shove Jamal. Not a single student came to Jamal's defense. He continued to withdraw and began getting sick each day before school.

SHE SAID

In Jefferson Middle School there is a secret club for girls. The three girls who are in charge of the club are bossy and downright mean. These girls have been spreading vicious rumors and making ethnic slurs. They have targeted two students, Lakisha, who is African American, and Holly, who is of Asian descent. Lakisha and Holly frequently visit the nurse's office during their lunch hour with complaints of headaches, nausea, and dizziness. Teachers have never directly witnessed the verbal assaults, but they have received grievances from other students. Lakisha and Holly have been reluctant to report these episodes. Within the past 2 weeks, Lakisha has missed 5 school days. Holly has attended class but often appears distracted.

HE SAID

Ms. M., a seventh-grade teacher, overhears Johnny, Alan, and Sam discussing a situation in which a classmate is being bullied. They express their dismay in seeing this person bullied but are unsure about what they should do. Johnny thinks that if they intervene they will make it worse and cause the bully to turn on them. Alan thinks that they should stand up for the bullied person the next time it happens. Sam just doesn't know which idea is best.

An Afternoon at the Movies

OBJECTIVES

- To help students identify bully/victim scenarios in a broad range of contexts

- To encourage students to become aware of feelings associated with witnessing bullying interactions

- To promote insight into the behaviors of bullies and victims

- To help generate ideas on how to intervene in a bully/victim interaction

MATERIALS

- Videotaped movie of choice

- Movie Review worksheet

DIRECTIONS

1. Each of the following movies includes scenes where bullying takes place. Select one or substitute another that you think illustrates bullying and ways of dealing with bullying.

    The Karate Kid

    Grease

    Can't Buy Me Love

    Lucas

    Stand by Me

    Back to the Future

    Circle of Friends

    Rudy

    Pretty in Pink

    Sixteen Candles

    Dangerous Minds

    Jack

2. Show the scene to the students. (If time permits, you could show the entire video.)

3. Ask students to complete the Movie Review worksheet.

4. Facilitate a group discussion related to the students' responses on the worksheet. As you discuss, help students identify the ABC's of the scene, where A = the antecedent (what happened before and leading up to the incident); B = the behavior (the bullying behavior); and C = the consequence (the outcome for each person involved, both in the immediate situation and later on).

DISCUSSION

- What might have been done to prevent the bullying situation? (Challenge any answers that seem to be "blaming the victim" for what happened.)

- What different steps could the characters have taken during the bullying situation that would have made the outcome less damaging?

- Does this kind of situation happen at our school? If so, what could we do to prevent it or make the outcome less damaging?

NOTE

Familiarize yourself with the scene(s) you are going to show before presenting them to the group. You may also wish to give students a homework assignment to find examples of bullying behavior in movies or TV shows. (Be careful if you have students bring in videos; some material may be offensive or extreme.) The more subtle the events depicted, the more skill students will develop in identifying aggressive acts.

MOVIE REVIEW

1 **Who was the bully?**

_____

2 **What made him/her the bully?**

_____

_____

_____

_____

3 **Who was the victim?**

_____

4 **Why did the bully pick on this person?**

_____

_____

_____

_____

5 **What did the victim do in response to the bullying?**

_____

_____

_____

_____

6 **Can you think of any other scenes from movies or TV that you think depict bullying or victimization? Please list them, and say what scene(s) in particular you think are good examples.**

_____

_____

_____

_____

_____

_____

_____

_____

_____

_____

On the Outside, Looking In

OBJECTIVES

- To help students gain an understanding of the behaviors, feelings, and thoughts of both bullies and victims

- To provide a safe environment for students to discuss and express their feelings, thoughts, and opinions about bullies and victims

MATERIALS

- A chair
- Chalkboard or easel pad

DIRECTIONS

1. Ask students to sit in a circle. Place an empty chair inside the circle.

2. Invite students to imagine a bully sitting in the chair, then to describe the characteristics and behaviors of the bully.

3. Go around the circle and ask students to take turns telling the imaginary bully how they feel about him or her. It is important that the students articulate what they do not like, express why they feel the bully acts in this manner, and say how they could assist the bully in changing his or her behavior. As the students discuss, write their main points on the chalkboard or easel pad.

4. If time permits, repeat the procedure, but ask students to imagine a victim in the middle of the circle. Invite them to describe how they feel about the behaviors directed toward the victim, how they could provide support to the victim, and how the victim could cope with the bullying.

5. Referring to the students' main points as appropriate, process the activity by discussing the following questions.

DISCUSSION

- Why do bullies do what they do?

- How do bullies see their behavior? Why?

- How do you see their behavior? Why?

- Did we develop thoughts on how to help bullies change? What are they?

- What should we as a class or group be doing to help reduce bullying? What steps should we be taking?

NOTE

This can be a very emotional activity. Take care that no one is made fun of during the exercise. Stress the concepts of respect and dignity when talking about both victims and bullies.

MODULE

3 Recognizing the Victim

OVERVIEW

Every day thousands of children fall prey to aggressive acts by peers. As children, we commonly hear the refrain "Sticks and stones will break my bones, but names will never hurt me." Nevertheless, name-calling appears to be the most prevalent and devastating to its recipients (Besag, 1989), and it frequently leads to an escalation of aggression, often resulting in physical assault. Victims also have described bullying as including such behaviors as teasing, ridiculing, vandalizing property, and being physically violent (Hoover et al., 1992). The effects of such victimization are far reaching and expand into adulthood, severely traumatizing both boys and girls. This trauma has been linked to depression, helplessness, and even suicide. School shooting incidents have even been tied to victims' seeking retaliation. The children who are victimized are often the "forgotten group." Teachers and students, and even the majority of the academic literature, focus on half of the bully/victim interaction: the bully. The bully is the one who catches our attention. The victim, however, is likely to go unnoticed. At times, the victim is even blamed for being the object of the bully's aggression. This module will assist you in understanding the victim and the victim's role in the bully/victim interaction.

GOALS

- To increase awareness of the effects of victimization

- To challenge common myths about victims and victimization

- To recognize the characteristics of victims and the signs of victimization

- To identify different types of victims: passive, provocative, and bystander

- To differentiate male and female victims

- To break the "code of silence" surrounding bullying and victimization

EFFECTS OF VICTIMIZATION

When I was a young boy, the bully called me names, stole my bicycle, forced me off the playground. I was victim to the ridicule he heaped on me. He made fun of other children, forced me to turn over my lunch money each day, threatened to give me a black eye if I told adult authority figures. At different times I was subjected to a wide range of degradation and abuse—"de-pantsing," spit in my face, forced to eat playground dirt. . . . As I entered adolescence, I noticed that the bully could replicate himself. As part of male rites of passage, all boys were presented with a simple choice: suffer daily humiliation or join the ranks of the bully. We all had to answer the question, "Which side are you on?" I watched sweet childhood friends become hard and mean. I saw other sissy boys become neighborhood toughs. They formed gangs of bullies that tormented us. I witnessed the cycle of abuse which ensures the constant creation of new bullies and I vowed that this would never happen to me. Watching the powerless take on the trappings of power, I'd shake my head and withdraw into deeper isolation. . . . The world of children was a cruel place for me. (Rofes, 1994, pp. 37–38)

Victims are children who are exposed, often repeatedly and over time, to negative actions on the part of one or more bullies; they are teased, intimidated, threatened, degraded, dominated, hit, and kicked (Olweus, 1993). The effects of victimization are far reaching and can expand long beyond childhood years, with long-lasting consequences for the victims. The following list includes just some of the effects of victimization:

- Change in school performance

- Absenteeism

- Truancy

- Drop-out

- Peer rejection

- Fear and avoidance of social situations

- Feelings of alienation and loneliness

- Low morale

- Chronic illness

- Running away

- Poor self-confidence and self-esteem

- Depression

- Suicide

MYTHS AND REALITIES OF VICTIMIZATION

Erroneous beliefs about victims and victimization are common. Unfortunately, such myths sometimes prevent teachers from perceiving the situation in their own classrooms and schools accurately and from intervening. Some of these myths—and their associated realities—are as follows:

Myth: Sometimes kids ask for it. The way a child looks or acts attracts the bully. If the kid would just walk (or talk or dress, etc.) in a regular way, this wouldn't be happening.

Reality: No child asks to be bullied. Each child is doing the best he or she can and does not deserve to be victimized. Some children may act or look a certain way that attracts bullying; our job is to address the bullying and to help the victim learn skills to handle the bullying more effectively.

Myth: Sometimes bullies are actually helping victims by pushing them to learn to stand up for themselves.

Reality: Fear is not conducive to learning to stand up for oneself. We must teach kids the skills they need to be assertive in an understanding and supportive environment, not through coercion and threats.

Myth: Students will outgrow victimization. Victimization usually ends when a student enters high school, often after his or her freshman year.

Reality: The effects of victimization are profound and may reach into adulthood. The severe traumatization of victimized individuals has been linked to depression, helplessness, and, in some cases, suicide. We can prevent victimization by identifying the warning signs of victimization and by understanding the lasting effects of victimization.

Bullying is such a big problem. . . . I can't change it, so there is no sense trying.

—Seventh-grade teacher

Myth: It's been going on for a year. What is the big deal now? The kid can just keep handling it.

Reality: Just because people have endured a painful situation does not make the situation right. The cumulative effect of being harassed can be overwhelming. Any bullying incident can be the "straw that breaks the camel's back," causing illness, school avoidance, and even violence if the victimized child strikes back.

Oftentimes I know my teacher can't change the situation, but knowing that she cares is enough to get me through the tough times.

—Sixth-grade student

Myth: Only boys who are effeminate and small are bullied; only girls who are insecure and overweight are bullied.

Reality: Victimization is not limited to those students who exude characteristics of passivity (caution, sensitivity, quietness, anxiety, insecurity). Some are "provocative victims" and have particular behaviors that instigate bullying. We need to help these students learn and gain positive reinforcement for engaging in more appropriate behaviors.

Myth: As a teacher, the best thing I can do is take the victim aside for a private talk.

Reality: We need to put values out there and discuss them within our classrooms so witnesses to bullying also feel supported and recognize the efforts we are taking to help stop victimization.

Myth: Students are not sharing that they are being bullied, so I assume everything is OK.

Reality: This "code of silence" makes students fearful to tell authorities that they are being victimized or have witnessed another student being bullied. As teachers, it is our responsibility to break the code of silence and invite open communication in our classrooms.

Myth: If I encourage students to come talk to me, they will all start whining and telling on one another. Listening to peer problems will become the majority of my day.

Reality: There may be an initial increase in students who want to talk. However, when the problems begin being solved, you can start to move to a whole-class, solution-focused discussion, which will prevent further problems and "tattling."

Myth: I don't have time to address each small problem in my classroom.

Reality: Problems will escalate all year if not addressed early. Building problem solving and conflict resolution into the curriculum early will prevent severe problems later in the year and in following years.

RECOGNIZING VICTIMS AND VICTIMIZATION

Bullying requires a victim and ongoing events that inflict harm. Just who are the victims of bullying? And how, when victimization is uncommonly reported, can you recognize when it is happening?

Characteristics of Victims

Although each situation is different, the following example illustrates a common pattern of victimization. Have you seen this type of situation in your own classroom? What do you think caused this particular child to be targeted?

> *Jamal's family had to move from New Jersey to Georgia when he was in the sixth grade. Jamal was small, less developed than most of the boys in his new class, and lacked physical ability for sports and games. He appeared timid and withdrawn when he entered school. On his first day, Rodney, a large, boisterous classmate, began teasing Jamal about the way he talked, making fun of Jamal's accent and calling him a queer. Jamal began to cry, which provoked Rodney to become even*

more aggressive. Rodney told the other students he was
right because queers cry a lot and are sissies. This
caused the other students to laugh and tease Jamal.
Each day the taunting and teasing increased, and sever-
al of the boys began to push, trip, and shove Jamal.
None of the students came to Jamal's defense. He contin-
ued to withdraw and began getting sick each day before
school.

It's not always the victim's fault. . . . Sometimes it is, though.

—13-year-old boy

In general, children who become targets of bullying exhibit the following kinds of characteristics:

- Lack the social skills required for peer interaction

- React negatively to conflicts or losing

- Seek comfort from adults in times of conflict

- Manifest behavior patterns of crying and anxiety

- Possess certain characteristics or mannerisms that mark them as vulnerable

- Demonstrate low levels of popularity and have few friends (Slee & Rigby, 1993)

- Are cautious, sensitive, quiet, anxious, and insecure

I know we shouldn't pick on Billy, but he walks and talks just like a girl and my brother says he prances down the halls. I like him, but he just cries when we tell him to quit acting faggy. The teacher ought to tell him how to be when he's at school.

—Sixth-grade boy

At times you may have difficulty identifying why certain children in your classroom are targeted. Perhaps the best way to identify victims is to ask them directly. Other students may have a better understanding of what leads to the victimization; the victim's peers can often share information you have missed, or the bullies themselves can often describe what it is about a person that leads to the desire to be aggressive. Also, talk with your professional peers. Together, you may be able to gain insight in order to provide the assistance the victim needs.

Each child has a right to his or her individuality, and all children deserve respect and to be treated with dignity. Yet the very characteristics that cause us to notice children who may be different may be the same that result in their being bullied and victimized by peers.

While many children have elected to be "different" and even thrive on their individuality, we have known many children who just didn't know how they were perceived or that they could do anything about characteristics that brought ridicule from peers. This is a difficult balance: how to avoid "blaming the victim," at the same time supporting and encouraging change if the child desires. The role of counselors and teachers is to help children learn more effective ways of living: We do this through a combination of teaching acceptance in the classroom and facilitating individual change if that is what the child wants. We can work with these children to help them consider ways to deflect bullying and manage the reactions of others—for example, developing prosocial skills that allow them to use humor and assertion, or cultivating a cadre of peers who will become involved to help. Some children also may be interested in learning how to appear "less different" in terms of apparel, mannerisms, or other characteristics.

Secondary Signs of Victimization

Teachers have shared with us that they do not dismiss victimization intentionally. In fact, if they do not witness the event, they may have few or only subtle cues that it is taking place. Some of the *secondary signs* of victimization, criticial to identification and intervention, are as follows:

- An unusually quiet child becomes increasingly withdrawn.

- A child who is normally restrained becomes aggressive (as a result of frustration and inability to cope with the victimization in other ways).

- A student's school performance deteriorates without apparent reason.

- A child is reluctant to be involved in recess or extracurricular group activities.

- A child becomes ill prior to group-related activities.

- During group activities, no one wants to be paired with this individual.

- The child is absent without a convincing explanation.

- The child's personal property is damaged or missing on a regular basis.

- A child begins skipping lunch or asking to eat lunch somewhere other than in the cafeteria.

If you begin to notice any of these signs in a child, make yourself available to him or her. You might say, for example, "Sarah, I have noticed that you have become very quiet over the last week and haven't turned in your homework assignments. It seems as though something may be bothering you. Would you like to talk about it? It is safe with me." Explore possible explanations for change in behavior. Be active in identifying what may be going on and who the best person to help might be—sometimes it will be you, but it also may be a counselor, social worker, school psychologist, or someone else on the school staff. Victims need to know someone believes in them and is willing to help.

It is especially important that teachers not simply accept children's physical complaints at face value but delve into reasons for these physical complaints. The following scenario illustrates a rather common sequence of events:

> *Anna despised lunch hour. Since day one of the school year, Anna was continually tormented by three other girls at lunch time. After 2 weeks of being the butt of the girls' mockery, Anna began to feel ill just as the lunch*

*hour rolled around. On Monday, Anna asked if she could
have a hall pass to go to the nurse's station. She com-
plained of a stomachache and headache. On Tuesday,
during lunch, Anna asked if she could see the nurse
because her throat was sore. On Wednesday, Anna did
not show up for school at all.*

TYPES OF VICTIMS

Just as there are different forms of bullying, there are different types of
victims: passive, provocative, and bystander. Each group has particular
difficulties and needs.

Passive Victims

Passive victims, also referred to as *submissive victims,* try to avoid conflict by staying out of harm's way. They frequently have emotional out-
bursts (e.g., crying) in response to the fear and frustration of being
bullied. Their behaviors often indicate to others that they are weak and
therefore incapable of retaliation when attacked or insulted (Olweus,
1993). Passive victims share the following characteristics:

- Most frequently targeted (Olweus, 1993)

- Abandoned and isolated at school

- More anxious and insecure than peers (Ross, 1996)

- Cautious, sensitive, and quiet

- Often lack physical ability comparable to those of their tormentors

- Possess low self-esteem—may see themselves as unattractive and
  failures

- Often do not share a solid friendship with a single child in the class

- Demonstrate close, overprotective relationships with parents, especially mothers

Interviews with parents of male passive victims reveal that these
boys often exhibited characteristics of cautiousness and sensitivity at
an early age. These attributes, when combined with physical weakness,
are likely to contribute to these children's victimization, inasmuch as
they are unable to stand up for and assert themselves in the peer
group. The tendency toward overprotection by parents, especially mothers, is considered both a cause and consequence of bullying.

Passive victims may be difficult to recognize because they are
unlikely to come forth to ask for help, and their torment may appear
superficially to be the result of childhood teasing. However, perpetual
taunting affects these youths' self-esteem and their ability to perform in
the academic setting. As Rofes (1994) notes:

The abuse I suffered in the American public schools from kindergarten to my senior year of high school created deep psychic scars with which I have struggled throughout my lifetime. These same scars are shared by many others. We will never forget that we were tortured and publicly humiliated. (pp. 37–38)

Provocative Victims

A second category of victims includes provocative victims, who, as bullies would say, actively "ask" for their abuse. Provocative victims are distinguished from passive victims by the fact that they, like bullies, are also aggressive (Pellegrini, 1998). Sometimes called *reactive bullies,* these youth tend to instigate trouble deliberately to provoke others, accepting this behavior over being ignored (Besag, 1989). Bullies tend to take it upon themselves to "educate" these victims on the group's values and ways (Olweus, 1993, 1994).

Provocative victims share the following characteristics:

- Less common than passive victims

- More active, assertive, and confident than passive victims (Ross, 1996)

- More likely to create management problems within the classroom

- At higher risk for negative developmental outcomes (e.g., peer rejection and suicide; Pellegrini, 1998)

- Unpopular among peers but often do not suffer from low self-esteem

- May associate with bullies to increase their social status (Boulton & Smith, 1994)

- Receive positive reinforcement from bullies in the form of attention

- May learn aggressive strategies by imitating bullies' actions and employing these tactics with their less dominant peers

Provocative victims are particularly deserving of attention because they are the most rejected members of their peer group (Perry, Kusel, & Perry, 1988). This rejection is what places them at increased risk for negative developmental outcomes, including suicide.

These children would like not to be victims, but it seems that they just do not know how to get along with other kids.

—Middle-school counselor

You may be asking yourself why provocative victims continue to engage in behaviors that appear to cause them nothing but trouble. Some teachers confess they have difficulty understanding these youths. It is important to think beyond these youths' most immediate behavior to their environment and to the ways they have learned to use these specific types of behavior. Our experience with provocative victims is that they often have been bullied in their homes and neighborhoods, like the recognition they receive from the individuals they provoke, lack prosocial skills for getting along with peers, and feel that the negative attention and even painful experiences they encounter are preferable to being ignored.

Provocative victims often lack adequate anger management skills. Although we generally think of anger management as a skill to be taught to bullies to reduce aggression toward their victims, it is also important to be aware of the role unmanageable anger plays for victims. Most individuals' anger builds on a continuum. On a scale of 1 to 10, with 10 being the highest, anger generally builds through the following stages.

STAGES OF ANGER DEVELOPMENT

- **Stage 1**   Slightly bothered

- **Stage 2**   Becoming more aware of the problem

- **Stage 3**   Wishing the problem would stop

- **Stage 4**   Beginning to think of ways to get out of the situation

- **Stage 5**   Experiencing flushing or other manifestations of a "fight or flight" reaction

- **Stage 6**   Becoming more aroused and actively seeking to reduce provocation

- **Stage 7**   Speaking loudly and moving toward a defensive/aggressive stance

- **Stage 8**   Preparing to take steps necessary to gain superiority in the interaction

- **Stage 9**   Believing the situation requires full commitment

- **Stage 10** Full rage and both emotional and physical response

The ability to become aware of the developmental stages of anger and take steps to reduce escalation or remove oneself from the situation is a developmental task, a function of maturity. Many provocative victims go through the first stage or two of the anger process, then jump immediately to Stage 10, full rage. There is no gradual buildup of anger. The provocative victim has no time to think; rather, he or she acts quickly and impulsively. This rapid escalation of anger from the initial stages of anger to full-blown fury can be effective in reducing victimization, to the extent that bullies react with fear when they see someone behaving unpredictably and aggressively.

In provocative victims the release of anger may be extreme, resulting in anything from yelling to throwing furniture and aggressive acting out to even more violent activities, such as those we have seen recently involving students acting out with weapons in schools.

When we talk with provocative victims, they explain that they do not intend to lose control but that when harassed or picked on they become extremely frightened, see no way to defend themselves, then lose all semblance of control over their feelings and behavior. Clearly, one of our goals is to help such students recognize the anger continuum and teach them more effective ways to release their anger.

Bystander Victims

The bully/victim interaction affects numerous youth, even those not directly involved in the interaction. These individuals are the bystander victims. These youth may observe bullying on a continual basis. Although they are not bullied directly, they are forever impacted by the abuse they witness. They often feel guilty for not reporting these incidents—even that they are "cowards" or "weak" because they are not adequately equipped with the skills or resources to intervene. These individuals can develop "learned helplessness," or a sense that they are powerlessness to have an impact in their own or others' lives.

Bystanders may not report or intervene in bullying incidents for a number of reasons, chiefly the following:

- Insensitivity to the distress the bullying is causing

- Fear that they might be the bully's next target

- Previous experiences of reporting incidents and adults' inability or unwillingness to help

- Attributing the problem to the individual targeted by the bully (i.e., blaming the victim)

Bystander victims are truly presented with a "no-win situation": If they stand up for the victim, they may place themselves at risk of becoming the next victim; if they remain silent, they may carry guilt for many years. Bullying that is witnessed and that goes unpunished also can create a climate of apprehension, counterproductive to the goals of learning.

MALE AND FEMALE VICTIMS

Within each of the three categories, both male and female victims are represented. Victims of aggression appear to be subjected to different types of bullying behavior on the basis of their sex.

In general, boys experience physically aggressive bullying more often than girls (Hoover et al., 1992). They also experience violent and threatening behavior more often than girls (e.g., shoving, hitting; Sharp & Smith, 1991). In contrast, girls experience verbal bullying more often than boys, as well as more social bullying (e.g., rejection or isolation from the peer group). It is important to note, however, that in recent years, females increasingly have both perpetrated and been the victims of physical bullying. In males, the victimization may begin in a verbal form and immediately progress to an aggressive interaction.

> Male bullies tend to attribute victimization to the victim: Bullying is brought upon the person by himself. . . . "He might start acting smart and the group might keep on slugging him and hitting him." (Mellor, 1990, p. 5, quoting a 14-year-old boy)

> *American society stresses independence and power. These beliefs permeate individuals at all ages; however, youth are not often prepared mentally or physically to cope with the aggression of bullies. Teachers are in perfect positions to model collaborative problem solving and help-seeking behaviors.*
>
> *—Eighth-grade teacher*

As we have discussed, victims often neglect to report incidents to school officials for fear of retaliation, and, when they do, support from school authorities is often minimal or nonexistent. When questioned, teachers say they feel powerless and unskilled to handle bullying situations, therefore in most cases leaving the child to his or her own defenses or hoping that peers will intervene. Bystanders often fail to protect their peers because they fear they will draw the bully's attention to themselves, feel ill-equipped to intervene, or see the situation as none of their business.

Mottoes such as "Stand up for yourself" and "Don't be a tattletale" are messages that often prevent children from seeking help when they are victimized. Few things can be more damaging for a child than to confide in someone he or she believes can help and to be rejected or receive only temporary assistance. When this happens, the victim's fundamental fear that the bully will intensify the harassment often comes to pass. Victims feel even more frightened and isolated than before (Bryne, 1994a, 1994b).

As a teacher, you are in a unique position to witness and intervene in bullying. Because victims typically do not ask for help, it is up to you to reach out to students in need. By establishing an "open door policy" and encouraging students to discuss the bully/victim dilemma within the classroom environment, you can help students begin to feel more confident in seeking adult support. Often youth, particularly bystanders, want to intervene but simply do not have the skills to do so. With your encouragement, bystanders can become empowered to come forth and solicit your aid. It may be helpful to establish a confidential drop box where students can safely deposit notes describing the bullying incidents they witness. Together, you and your class can develop other creative solutions to overcome the bullying problem.

CONTENT REVIEW

The following statements refer to the learning goals of this module. Take a minute to think about the statements. Ask yourself whether you feel confident that you can say yes to each. If not, please revisit those topics and consider ways to strengthen your learning.

I realize that victimization has long-lasting and severe effects on youths' development.	Yes ❏ No ❏
I can recognize secondary signs of victimization in my students.	Yes ❏ No ❏
When a child displays warning signs, or when I am told by another student that victimization is occurring, it is my responsibility to investigate the situation.	Yes ❏ No ❏
I understand that victims may not ask for help for fear of reprisals.	Yes ❏ No ❏

I understand that youth can be passive, provocative, or bystander victims. I am able to recognize and identify the behaviors of each type.

Yes ❏   No ❏

I am aware that both boys and girls are involved in the bullying interaction.

Yes ❏   No ❏

I understand that victimization of boys and girls can differ greatly. Typically, boys experience more aggressive bullying, whereas girls experience more passive (verbal and social) bullying.

Yes ❏   No ❏

I can aid students by creating an open environment where students feel comfortable to discuss their own or others' victimization.

Yes ❏   No ❏

I recognize that giving advice to "Toughen up" or "Don't tattle" can prevent children from seeking my help.

Yes ❏   No ❏

A Reminder . . .

CLASSROOM INTERACTION AND AWARENESS CHART

Use the CIAC to describe any bullying behavior you observe (and that students report to you, if you wish). Specific instructions for filling out the CIAC appear in Appendix D, along with a blank copy of the chart.

THE BIG QUESTIONS

Focus yourself and honestly appraise your progress by asking yourself the "Big Questions." There are no right or wrong answers.
With regard to victims of bullying behavior:

1. What is my goal?

2. What am I doing?

3. Is what I am doing helping me achieve my goal?

4. *(If not)* What can I do differently?

PERSONAL GOALS FORM

The Personal Goals Form, on the next page, is designed to help you tailor the content of this module to your own students and situation. If you have not filled out the form as you worked through the information component of the module, please take a moment to do so now.

Personal Goals Form

GOALS

- To increase awareness of the effects of victimization

- To challenge common myths about victims and victimization

- To recognize the characteristics of victims and the signs of victimization

- To identify different types of victims: passive, provocative, and bystander

- To differentiate male and female victims

- To break the "code of silence" surrounding bullying and victimization

1. My personal perceptions of a victim:

   _____

   _____

2. I have observed incidents of victimization in my classroom. *(Please record incidents on the Classroom Interaction and Awareness Chart. Specify under "Behaviors" whether the incidents involve passive, provocative, or bystander victims.)*

3. I will conduct the following classroom activities to help my students become more able to recognize victims:

   _____

   _____

4. I will evaluate the effectiveness of these activities by (a) recording incidents on the CIAC to see if there is a reduction across time, (b) monitoring the extent to which students report bullying situations, and (c) recording my impressions of change in the classroom environment. *(Please indicate any other means of evaluation in the space below.)*

   _____

   _____

5. I will give students feedback on their progress by (a) sharing the number and types of incidents recorded on the CIAC and (b) encouraging classroom discussion of these incidents and related issues. *(Please indicate any other means of giving feedback in the space below.)*

   _____

   _____

6. I will share my experiences in applying the information in this module with members of my Support Team, other teachers, administrators, parents. *(Please specify who and when in the space below.)*

   _____

   _____

Classroom Activities

PROUD TO BE ME

Designed to help students appreciate individual diversity, this activity serves as an excellent icebreaker. It allows students to interact with one another, expand beyond their immediate social group, and learn about classmates with whom they may not usually interact.

LEND ME YOUR EARS

Prevention of bullying requires many skills. This activity allows students to improve their listening skills while they share stories about victimization. Students are encouraged to empathize and recognize common experiences.

GET CRAFTY

This activity is great for incorporating discussions of bullying into academic areas. Students work independently and creatively on projects to increase their awareness of bullying and victimization, then present their projects to the class.

Proud to Be Me

OBJECTIVES

- To help students learn how they are different from their classmates
- To assist students in communicating with other students outside their immediate peer group
- To encourage students to appreciate individuality

MATERIALS

- Proud to Be Me worksheet
- Proud to be Different worksheet
- Chalkboard or easel pad

DIRECTIONS

1. Distribute copies of the Proud to Be Me worksheet, one per student.

2. Ask students to complete the statements on the worksheet by filling in the blanks with information about themselves.

3. After students have completed this worksheet, distribute the Proud to be Different worksheet.

4. Ask students to walk around the room and talk to their classmates about their responses on the Proud to Be Me worksheet. Students should search for classmates who have different responses to each question and record their answers on their Proud to be Different worksheet. If possible, it is best for them to have a different student respond to each question.

5. Conduct a class discussion on the differences among and variety of responses to each question. Write some of the responses on the chalkboard or easel pad so you can identify themes or topics of special interest to the class. Stress that, even though students have many similarities, their interests, backgrounds, and experiences may be quite different.

DISCUSSION

- What are some new things you learned today about members of your class?

- How did your interests compare with those of others? Which of your interests were the same? Which differed?

- Was your background the same or different? How so?

- What can we learn from this experience (that respecting peoples' differences is important; that we come from many backgrounds and that is OK).

NOTE

If your school has a program to increase sensitivity to diversity issues, you may want to ask teachers or others who are especially involved for materials that could be incorporated.

PROUD TO BE ME

Instructions: Fill in each blank with information about yourself.

1   I was born in _____.

2   I have _____ brothers and sisters.

3   My favorite movie is _____.

4   My cultural heritage is _____.

5   I want to be a _____ when I am older.

6   My favorite subject is _____.

7   I like to _____ after school.

8   I am happiest when _____.

9   My best characteristic is my _____.

10 I get really angry when _____.

11 My favorite color is _____.

12 If I were an animal I would be a _____.

13 It makes me laugh when _____.

14 It hurts my feelings when _____.

PROUD TO BE DIFFERENT

Instructions: Find a classmate whose response is different from your own on the Proud to Be Me worksheet. Write the person's name in the first blank and record his or her response in the second blank. If possible, get a different classmate to respond to each item.

1   _____ was born in _____ .

2   _____ has _____ brothers and sisters.

3   _____ 's favorite movie is _____ .

4   _____ 's cultural heritage is _____ .

5   _____ wants to be a _____ .

6   _____ 's favorite subject is _____ .

7   _____ likes to _____ after school.

8   _____ is happiest when _____ .

9   _____ 's best characteristic is _____ .

10 _____ gets really angry when _____ .

11 _____ 's favorite color is _____ .

12 If _____ were an animal, he/she would be a _____ .

13 It makes _____ laugh when _____ .

14 It hurts _____ 's feelings when _____ .

Lend Me Your Ears

OBJECTIVES

- To give students an opportunity to listen to the struggles of victims

- To help students practice listening to one another and experience being heard

- To enhance students' awareness of others' feelings and beliefs

MATERIALS

- None

DIRECTIONS

1. Group students into pairs.

2. Have one student share an experience in which he or she was victimized. The student may share the details of the experience, emotions and feelings related to the experience, or thoughts about the experience. If the student finds it difficult to recall or prefers not to relate his or her own experience, then have the student share an experience that he or she has witnessed (no names, please).

3. Encourage the other member of the pair to describe, in his or her own words, the first member's struggle. Together, have them attempt to identify the ABC's of the situation, where A = the antecedent (what happened before and leading up to the incident); B = the behavior (the bullying behavior); and C = the consequence (the outcome for the person, both in the immediate situation and later on).

4. Invite pairs to switch roles and repeat Steps 2 and 3.

5. Conduct a discussion with the larger group, using the following questions as a guide.

DISCUSSION

- How did you feel as you heard your partner present the information you heard?

- How did it feel to talk to your partner about your own situation?

- What if anything did you notice about your partner's listening that was particularly helpful?

- What was it like to try to identify the ABC's of the situation?

- Did you discuss what might have happened to make the outcome better?

NOTE

Students sometimes exaggerate their stories, or they may share inappropriate information, such as family stories or incidents. It is important before beginning this activity to give school-based examples and set limits, then to move among the students as they talk to monitor their discussion.

Get Crafty

OBJECTIVE

- To provide an opportunity within the academic content areas for students to express their thoughts, feelings, and reactions about bullying and victimization

MATERIALS

- Varying, depending on the activity selected

DIRECTIONS

1. Select an idea in one of the following content areas to encourage students to express thoughts, feelings, and reactions related to bullying and victimization. (You can also "get crafty" and create your own method to facilitate students' expression.)

LANGUAGE ARTS ACTIVITY

Have students write a poem or short story about a bully and his or her victim, their own thoughts and feelings about bullying/victimization, and so on.

SOCIAL STUDIES ACTIVITY

Encourage students to write a fictional account to explain when and how they believe bullying/victimization commenced and/or to identify groups of people who have been bullied/victimized throughout history (e.g., Jewish people, slaves in the United States, Irish people immigrating to this country in the 1900s).

ART ACTIVITY

Ask students to draw pictures or create collages that represent bullying/victimization and express their feelings about bullying.

2. Have students present their projects to the class.

3. Conduct a class discussion of the students' experiences, including their reactions to the projects.

DISCUSSION

- What did you learn from doing your project?

- What did you learn from your classmates' presentations?

- How do you think this has affected you personally?

- How do you think you can use what you have learned to help your classmates and others reduce aggression and bullying in school?

NOTE

Your Support Team can help you brainstorm other activities to integrate the antibullying objective into the curriculum. You may also want to encourage students to involve their parents or other family members in their projects. Doing so will help students share some of the work they are doing at school to prevent and reduce bullying.

MODULE

4 Taking Charge: Interventions for Bullying Behavior

OVERVIEW

Now that you have gained a greater understanding of what bullying is and are able to identify the bullies and the victims, it is time to tackle the bullying that may be occurring in your classroom. Many techniques and interventions to address aggression in young people have been developed. This module will introduce several basic interventions, appropriate for all teachers working with all bullies. The focus is on approaches that have been found particularly useful in classroom and school settings and that are compatible with the teaching curriculum.

GOALS

- To learn the importance of an invitational approach in initiating contact and establishing rapport with bullies

- To learn the "Four R's" of bully control and some general strategies for intervening with bullies

- To understand basic behavior change principles as they relate to bullying

- To learn specific areas that can be developed in bullies to help them change their behaviors

- To learn interventions for bullies and victims together

- To understand how reputation plays a part in maintaining bullying behavior

INITIATING CONTACT AND ESTABLISHING RAPPORT

We all like to be nurtured, and a problem most bullies have is that they receive criticism or are ignored more often than they are nurtured. This means that they seek attention in the way they know best—by being aggressive. Most bullies are "walking wounded" in the sense that they have not received the emotional nurturance they so crave. A first step toward reaching out is to realize that, although you may find their behavior intimidating and problematic, these children need your help as much as victims do.

Central to rapport with bullies, as well as with other students, is an *invitational approach*. What we mean by an invitational approach is that we invite bullies to talk with us, explain their perceptions of the problem, provide any additional information they may have, and participate in developing a plan of action. This approach requires firmness, commitment, and willingness to listen. For example: "Marya, we need to talk. I would like you to talk with me about what is going on between you and Jessie. You see, I've got a problem, and that problem is I am responsible for everyone in this classroom, and the way you have been intimidating Jessie cannot continue. We have to find a way to fix this. I would like you to come to talk with me about this now."

Bullies often feel they are being singled out and treated unfairly, as the following dialogue shows:

Teacher: Randall, you deliberately pushed Scott. We don't do that in our school.

Randall: He pushed me. You always think I'm the one. Scott pushed me first. It just isn't fair how you always defend the little preppies.

Teacher: I agree, it seems I am on your case a lot, and it's also true that I do not fuss as much with some of the other students, like Scott. On the other hand, that is because I see you doing more things to bring harm to other students, and I can't let that happen. I like you, Randall, but this just can't keep happening. It is important for us to develop a plan so that you can keep being a leader with your friends but not hurt other people in the process.

Intead of telling Randall what he must do, the teacher reminds him of a rule that applies to everyone ("We don't do that in our school") and invites him to participate in developing a plan for change. A plan that involves the student's input is far more likely to be successful than one that does not.

THE FOUR R'S OF BULLY CONTROL

The key to successful bully prevention is to use what we call the "Four R's" of bully control:

1. **R**ecognize that a problem exists.

2. **R**emove yourself or step back from the situation if you do not feel you can effectively intervene.

3. **R**eview the situation.

4. **R**espond to the situation:

Module 4: Taking Charge—Interventions for Bullying Behavior

If you feel competent and confident to intervene, then do so.

If you are uncertain how to intervene, assist students in finding services elsewhere.

Using the Four R's can be very effective in managing bullying problems. This procedure is a variation on the Big Questions, discussed in the introduction to this book:

1. What is my goal? (The goal is to manage bullying behavior effectively. When a problem exists, it must be *recognized* and defined.)

2. What am I doing? (Examining what you are doing reflects how important it is to step back, to *remove* oneself from the conflict in order to understand the situation better.)

3. Is what I am doing helping me achieve my goal? (Asking this question allows us to *review* the situation to figure out whether what we have been doing is working to resolve the problem.)

4. *(If not)* What can I do differently? This fourth question relates to the way we *respond* to the situation—by intervening in the problem or referring it to someone else who has greater skills and expertise.

GENERAL INTERVENTION STRATEGIES

Following are some general strategies that may assist you in intervening in bullying situations in your classroom. Using these strategies can also have a preventive effect.

Take steps to create a positive environment
Part of creating a positive environment is considering the physical layout of your classroom: Do you seat students so several aggressive children are not together? Do you separate bullies and victims so that bullies cannot easily taunt or tease victims? Another part of a positive environment is the room itself—it should be arranged in an aesthetically pleasing way but not in a way students find distracting.

Establish and enforce classroom rules
Establish classroom rules early in the year and enforce them as consistently and fairly as possible. Have you involved students in a discussion of the rules so that they will feel ownership of them? The development of classroom rules is discussed at length in Module 6, "The Role of Prevention."

Act quickly to intervene
Do not ignore misbehavior. If you do, the bully may interpret your lack of response as permission. Instead, defuse the situation by confronting the bully immediately. It is important to intervene even in low-level bullying incidents. Do not allow low-level verbal or physical provocation to transpire because such behavior may become a habit. Further, we know from experience that if a bully is allowed to get away with small acts of aggression, the misbehavior will escalate until he or she is

finally required to stop. Classrooms should consider having "zero toler-ance" for aggression and violence. In other words, every incident of bul-lying, no matter how small, results in a sanction of some sort.

Use positive interpersonal skills with all students, even bullies

In interactions with bullies, it is best to use clear and succinct state-ments, have a firm and controlled voice, and maintain direct eye con-tact. When you say, "I want you to behave," you are not using clear, definitive language. However, when you say, "I want you to sit at your desk for the next 10 minutes, working on your social studies," you are much clearer in your communication. The use of "I want" in this latter statement clarifies that it is your expectation and not a question. In contrast, the question "Don't you want to sit down and do your work?" does not express the expectation as being yours. It also permits the stu-dent to answer no, which is something you don't want.

When you make direct eye contact, the student is unable to pretend that he or she did not hear you. Also, the use of direct eye contact con-notes authority, that you are in charge and expect the student to listen to you. Study your use of eye contact, for much is communicated in the process. It is important to realize, however, that students from some cultures are taught not to maintain eye contact with teachers, for that may be a sign of disrespect. Also, if eye contact becomes a staring con-test and is perceived as aggressive, the acting out can escalate.

Examine your own response to bullying incidents

Balance your support for victim and bully. Any indication of lack of sup-port to the victim could be perceived by the bully as permission for fur-ther attacks. However, an overly sympathetic response toward the victim (by teacher or classmates) could humiliate the victim or result in the bully's attempting to gain further negative attention by continuing to focus on the victim. Overly punitive responses may result in the bully's modeling your behavior or becoming increasingly vindictive.

Provide students with a way out of conflicts and confrontations

When students are in a confrontational situation, they often want to get out of it but do not know how to do so without "losing face" or looking cowardly. It is good to develop a repertoire of skills to help bullies find a way out of confrontations without looking like losers. If you corner a bully, everyone in the situation will lose.

Consider how the teacher in the following example intervenes: Malcolm got into a shoving match with Robert, who is much smaller and whom Malcolm had picked on previously. The teacher said to the aggressor:

> *Malcolm, I know you and Robert are having a disagree-ment, but in this classroom we don't push and shove. I need you to sit down now, and you, too, Robert. Later, when we are doing desk work, I need to talk with you.*

This response does not shame or blame. It does restate the rule ("In this classroom, we don't push and shove"). Ownership is with the teacher ("I need you to sit down now"), and it is clear that the teacher will not overlook the situation and that something will be done ("Later . . . I need to talk with you").

Let students know they are important and worth the effort to help learn new skills
Communicate to students that they are worth the time and energy you are putting forth. Explain that you are willing to work with them because you know that they are important and strong, but that they are using their strength in the wrong way, and you believe they have the capacity to learn to use it more effectively. The teacher in our previous example might say, for instance:

> *Malcolm, you were fighting with Robert. I'm not sure what it was about, but there are several things we need to talk about. First, we are clear about not causing hurt or pain to people, and you were hurting Robert. Second, you are much bigger than Robert, and while you are strong, you aren't using your strength in an appropriate manner—picking on other kids is not a good way to demonstrate your strength. Use your strength in sports activities, where you can help your team win. Third, I have great confidence in your being able to learn to handle conflicts better than you did today. I want us to explore some other things you can do instead.*

This would be an appropriate time and place to use the Big Questions with Malcolm, as listed under the discussion of the Four R's of bully control.

Empower students to take positive action against bullying
By explaining to all students that "We just don't do that here" we are also saying, "and you have permission to help me make sure it doesn't happen." This message must be conveyed in such a way that we do not instigate a vigilante attitude in our classes, in which students take on a mission to hurt and humiliate bullies. Our antibullying efforts should reduce pain and torment, not cause additional pain, even if it stops an undesirable behavior.

BEHAVIOR CHANGE PRINCIPLES

There are a number of strategies available for helping students learn more effective ways of interacting in the classroom and at school. Those next described are universal in their nature, appropriate for all students, useful throughout the classroom and school, and powerful in influencing students to change their behavior.

Before employing any specific behavior change strategies, however, consider your influence as a primary model for your students. Your students witness and monitor how you react in various situations and the behaviors you reinforce. You have an innate power to set precedents and guide behaviors in your classroom. Monitoring and altering your own behavior, if warranted, is the first step to take in facilitating change in the behaviors of your students.

Positive Reinforcement

Positive reinforcement, or just "reinforcement," is anything that causes a behavior to be maintained or increased. We sometimes hear a teacher say he or she used something as a reinforcer, such as smiley-face stickers or candy, but that the reinforcer did not work because the student's behavior did not improve. In that case, the object was not a reinforcer because it did not increase the desired behavior. The behavioral outcome determines whether something is reinforcing: To be reinforcing, the student must perceive it as such, regardless of how enticing someone else may think the item is. We once worked with a disruptive student, establishing a point system for appropriate behavior. When he accumulated enough points, he received a signed jersey from a famous basketball player, but he seemed disappointed. When asked why, he explained that the jersey was nice but that he did not like basketball. What he really wanted was some one-on-one time with the teacher. Teacher time was a stronger reinforcer than a jersey.

Types of Reinforcers

Reinforcers may take several forms. They may be part of a program, perhaps points that may be redeemed for something else later, or they may be more tangible—for instance, candy or a small toy. Reinforcers may also be social—for example, the teacher's praise or extra time for socializing with fellow students. Praise is the most important kind of social reinforcer. For example, a teacher might say something like the following:

- Sharice, I like it when you . . .

- Bob, I am proud of you for . . .

- Reshme, I noticed how hard you tried . . .

It is important always to use praise, or social reinforcement, when administering any other kind of reinforcer. If you are using an activity reinforcer to reward the entire class for going a certain length of time with no bullying incidents, you might say, for example, "Class, I am very proud of your behavior this week. Therefore, I am allowing you 15 minutes of extra computer time." Verbal praise is often not powerful enough when used initially. By combining praise with a tangible reward, the praise becomes more powerful and may become sufficient without the tangible reward.

Praise versus Encouragement

Praise and encouragement are two different concepts. Praise generally comes from the teacher and describes a characteristic that the teacher has noticed and about which the teacher feels good. As we have said, a teacher's praise is very powerful in getting a student's attention, identifying appropriate behavior, and encouraging positive behavior. A potential problem with teacher praise, though, is that it is external to the student: The student is inclined to behave in a particular way just to get the teacher to notice and give praise, not because the student wants to or feels like behaving that way.

With encouragement, the source of the reinforcement switches from external (the teacher) to internal (the student). When the teacher encourages, he or she is helping the student internalize the reinforcing message. For example:

- Monrose, you seemed really happy with how well you got that job done. I'll bet that makes you feel good.

- Van Tien, I encourage you to find a way you can manage that job with Carol. I'm sure you can do it.

- Carlos, you're working hard on the problem. You really seem to have a goal of accomplishing this—keep it up.

Guidelines for Using Reinforcement

In addition to using social reinforcement with all other types of reinforcement, the following guidelines will be helpful.

Reinforce the behavior you observe, not the child
For example, say, "John, I am proud of you for taking time to introduce Maureen to the other students." This tells John what you observed and liked, and provides him with feedback on what to do in the future.

Take the time to "catch them being good"
Reinforcement is designed to increase the behaviors you want more of, so find opportunities to let bullies know when they are engaging in appropriate behavior—let them know you notice and care. We have had numerous bullies tell us that the only time their teacher ever notices them is when they are "messing up," never when they are "doing things right." The bully's moral indignation over being treated unfairly can sometimes result in increased anger and misbehavior.

Create opportunities for bullies to feel good about themselves
Bullies have a history of being able to get attention only for misbehavior. In addition to catching them being good, we can plan programs or activities in which these students engage with others, have positive experiences, and receive teacher praise and encouragement for new skills and behaviors. Find out what these students excel in and encourage or provide opportunities for them to engage in these specified tasks (e.g., being a group leader, organizing a class party). Commenting to the class on the leadership abilities of a child who bullies may be helpful, though this must be done in a way that does not grant the bully additional power over others. Victims will be observing you carefully: It is important to help children who bully find prosocial roles without condoning their aggressive behavior.

Provide reinforcement as quickly and consistently as possible

Although adults and even some students who are more mature are used to delayed gratification, bullies generally are not very good at putting off reinforcement. When you decide that you are going to seek opportunities to reinforce the behaviors you want from a bully, you must reinforce frequently and consistently, especially at the beginning, or the student will lose confidence in your efforts. It is also important to reinforce the nonbullying behavior of bystanders and victims because you want the bully to want what the others are getting: positive attention and support from you as the teacher. The bully must understand that he or she will not receive your attention while behaving aggressively.

Attend to nonbullying behaviors

Seek opportunities to encourage on-task behavior, helping behaviors, assertive/nonaggressive behaviors, positive attending, and the like. Use social reinforcers such as praise as well as tangible rewards to reinforce the absence of negative behaviors and, especially, cooperative work with other students.

Removing Positive Reinforcement

Because one reason bullies behave as they do is to get attention, a way to reduce bullying behavior is to reduce the amount of reinforcement, specifically attention, that they get for being aggressive. One suggestion for making bullying less reinforcing is to discourage other students from laughing at or provoking students who bully. Other students' attention only adds fuel to the fire.

You can also wait until after class to confront a bully. If you do so, you avoid giving the bully class time in which all the other students watch your attention being directed toward the problem. When a teacher attends to a bully in front of the whole class, it demonstrates the bully's ability to pull the teacher into the confrontation, thereby giving the bully a sense of control. For a bully, your criticism is better than no attention at all. He or she would rather have you take up time with the whole class than be ignored. The bottom line is not to reinforce attention-seeking behavior.

A Peer-Support Model

Reinforcement within a peer-support model can be very effective. In this case, the group or class may receive a reward or benefit if the entire group works together to accomplish a task—in this case, to behave cooperatively. One way to involve the entire class is to divide the class into two or more groups. Each group begins with 20 points, written on the chalkboard. When a member breaks a classroom rule or commits an undesirable act, his or her group loses one point. The group with the most points left on the board at the end of the class period, day, or other span of time receives a reward.

Being a member of a team can be a powerful incentive for bullies to cease their bullying behaviors, for they then have the opportunity for positive interactions with their classmates. The difficulty with this approach, though, is that if the bully decides to be uncooperative, he or she has the ability to put the entire group at a disadvantage, and this could actually be reinforcing for a bully who does not care what happens to the group. He or she could derive a sense of power from holding all the others back from achieving the goal.

Punishment

Punishment is any consequence that results in the reduction of a behavior. As with reinforcement, punishment is determined by the outcome of the behavior: If a behavior is reduced or eliminated, then the consequence was punishing. Sometimes we think we are being punishing when, in fact, we are reinforcing the behavior we want changed. For example, one teacher decided to use a time-out procedure, removing a child from the classroom and having him sit at a desk in the hallway each time he misbehaved. The first time it worked—the student was more cooperative when he returned from the time-out period. Soon, though, the child learned he could have a great time sitting in the hallway watching other students go by and talking with the hall monitor, who would walk up and say things like "Wow, you out here again? You must be a bad dude. What did you do today?" The student would then tell elaborate stories about the tricks he had pulled. Clearly, the student was enjoying sitting in the hall more than classroom tasks, and his in-class misbehavior actually increased rather than decreased. To determine whether a consequence is punishing, the behavior should be decreasing.

Types of Punishment

Overcorrection, loss of privileges, and consequences are commonly used punishments. *Overcorrection* involves having the child overcompensate for harm done by practicing a positive behavior (e.g., if a student slams a door, have that student practice opening and closing the door 20 times). Overcorrection has two components: practicing the appropriate or right way to behave in the situation and making the situation better than it was by apologizing, doing something to make amends, or cleaning up a mess if making it was part of the misbehavior.

Loss of privileges can be effective when other methods—for example, time-out—do not work well. A student may find his or her misbehavior worth the time spent in a time-out room. On the other hand, the loss of a privilege—extracurricular activity time, taking a field trip, playground time, and so forth—often results in change. Because students place great value on these privileges, the threat of losing them is often sufficient to reduce or eliminate the misbehavior. Privileges are earned by appropriate behavior; it is important that students understand that privileges may be re-earned by behaving well.

Consequences are the privileges that are lost as the direct result of misbehavior. It is recommended that consequences for unacceptable behaviors be predetermined and identified at the beginning of the school year, clearly communicated to students, and carried out consistently. Note, however, that if a student does not value the privilege that will be lost, implementing the consequence will be of little value. Hence, an alternative consequence should be employed.

SPECIFIC AREAS OF DEVELOPMENT FOR BULLIES

Because bullies may be lacking in their development, they can benefit from specific instruction in a number of areas. Cognitive retraining, empathy skills training, social skills training, anger control training, and problem-solving training are possible approaches toward change. Your school counseling staff may be able to conduct a workshop or provide more information about these approaches.

Cognitive Retraining

Extensive research by Dodge (Dodge & Coie, 1987) and others has demonstrated that nonaggressive children are inclined to attribute an unintentional bump, slight shove, or tactless comment as accidental. Bullies, on the other hand, tend to attribute those activities to malice by others and believe they have both a right and an obligation to retaliate, even when objective observers are clear the intention was not to harm (Ross, 1996). In brief, cognitive retraining involves teaching bullies to view others' motivations in a more neutral way.

Empathy Skills Training

Empathy involves taking another person's perspective (i.e., understanding what another person is thinking and feeling) and caring about that person's experiences. Ideally, students learn through their early social experiences in the family and community to be respectful and treat others with dignity and caring, and to be empathic toward others. As we all know, that does not happen for a number of children. Bullies generally have not developed the cognitive skill of perspective taking, nor do they automatically care about others.

The ability to be empathic works to prevent aggressive responses in two ways. First, empathy and aggression are incompatible interpersonal responses. This means that becoming more skilled in the former helps diminish the latter (Goldstein, 1999). Second, responding to another individual in an empathic manner decreases or inhibits one's potential for acting aggressively toward the other.

Fortunately, students can learn to be more empathic. As for other behaviors, modeling of appropriate caring behaviors by teachers and other students can be quite influential. Activities to encourage empathy also need to be part of an intentional learning program. A number of the classroom activities in Appendix A deal with empathic awareness; the activity "All Ears" includes the "Teacher's Empathy Educator," an information guide for teaching students the definition of empathy and the key components in being empathic with others. Role-plays and role-reversals may be especially useful in helping a bully learn what it feels like to be the victim. In an initial *role-play,* two students act out a bully/victim scenario, expressing the thoughts, words, and feelings of each party. After the students have role-played the scenario, they practice *role-reversal*—in other words, the bully takes the part of the victim and vice versa. This procedure requires role-players to identify with another individual in order to react as that person would and encourages the bully to examine the victim's side and to understand the victim's feelings.

Social Skills Training

Ideally, a student observes appropriate social skills at home and in the classroom, recognizes how and why the behaviors are appropriate, and then masters them. However, more often an unskilled student fails to be aware of the behaviors or understand why they are important. Social skills are learned, and some students lack appropriate training (Goldstein & McGinnis, 1997; McGinnis & Goldstein, 1997).

Students can learn new social skills and increase their use of them given encouragement, support, and a proper learning environment. Briefly, teaching new skills involves the following steps:

1. Identifying the skill to be taught

2. Evaluating the current level of the skill

3. Breaking the skill into a sequence of smaller steps

4. Providing learning models (e.g., peers, television, films, books) that demonstrate the steps

5. Allowing sufficient time and opportunity for practice

6. Providing support and encouragement for use of the new skills

7. Monitoring use of the new skills and providing ongoing encouragement

Although we know teachers do not have time to run social skills groups in their classrooms each day, you may have time at the beginning of each class to share some suggestions. *Group-entry skills* are important for bullies and victims alike. The steps for entering a group may be discussed in class, then printed out on index cards and distributed to students. Then whenever a social entry situation arises, you can refer to the steps.

1. When approaching a group of students, watch and wait before joining in the conversation.

2. Listen and follow the conversation rather than introducing new topics.

3. Ask relevant questions and make comments.

4. Imitate the behavior of the group.

Anger Control Training

Interventions can be aimed at teaching bullies means other than physical force to control events. One way of doing this is to teach bullies to replace aggressive responses with assertive, constructive ones. Anger Control Training, a program developed by Goldstein, Glick, and Gibbs (1998), helps students learn to recognize their anger triggers and to apply techniques to reduce their anger. Students can be taught the physical cues (e.g., pounding heart, muscle tension, clenched fists) and thinking processes that lead to aggressive responses.

Anger triggers can be external (e.g., being pushed or shoved, being called a name) or internal (e.g, thinking, "That little jerk is making a fool of me—I'm going to kick his behind"). An external trigger often sets off a series of negative internal messages, the end result being aggression. The key to reducing aggressive acts, then, is to teach bullies how to substitute positive thoughts for negative thoughts as well as to recognize the physical cues associated with anger.

As discussed in Module 3, provocative victims often go through the stages of anger development very quickly. The same is true for bullies. Teaching them to stop before they reach full-blown anger and aggression is therefore very important.

Problem-Solving Training

Problem-solving training can help bullies see alternatives to solving a problem with aggression (see Shure, 1992a, 1992b, 1992c). The steps in the problem-solving process are as follows:

1. Stop and think.

2. Define the problem.

3. Generate alternative solutions.

4. Evaluate consequences of solutions.

5. Select a solution.

6. Implement the solution.

7. Evaluate the solution.

The Big Questions, discussed earlier in this module in relation to the Four R's of bully control, are a problem-solving process. You can encourage problem solving by using the Big Questions as a whole-class exercise and having all students participate in the process, but you can also apply the questions on a one-on-one basis whenever necessary. The following dialogue illustrates this process.

Teacher: Rick, what do you want? What is your goal?

Rick: I don't know what you mean.

Teacher: My goal is for all students to get along in class, to treat one another with respect and dignity, and to learn the material I have to teach. When you are bullying the others you aren't showing them respect and dignity, and you are interfering with their learning as well as yours.

Rick: Well, I don't mean to cause trouble, but it just keeps happening; they get in my face and really bug me.

Teacher: OK, so you have a goal of getting along. Right? So that's a goal compatible with my goal. That's great. Next question: What are you doing? The answer seems to be you are getting into fights and pushing several of the other students around. When you do this, does that help you achieve your goal?

Rick: Well, no, but they shouldn't tick me off either. They do it with their blasted "holier than thou" stuff they do—they just look at me like I'm stupid or something.

Teacher: You are not stupid, but you do get provoked. When you are provoked, does that help you achieve your goal of getting along?

Rick: No, but what else can I do?

Teacher: Great question. What else can you do?

Rick: I don't know. I do what I know, and that isn't working. You just said so.

Teacher: Right. I've got some suggestions for other things you might try. One alternative might be to practice ignoring the looks they give you. Another might be to tell them that when they look at you like that, you feel hurt because it seems they don't like you. Let's try these out and see if they will work.

INTERVENTIONS FOR BULLIES AND VICTIMS TOGETHER

According to Besag (1989), bullying is a two-sided problem. Although we will address interventions for victims separately, in the next module, we will present some ideas here for working with bullies and victims together.

Using a Solution-Focused Approach

As discussed in the introduction to this manual, many people identify a problem and focus on what caused the problem, how it manifests itself, and how awful it is. The *problem-focused approach*:

- Looks for the reason for the problem

- Tries to reduce the problem

- Looks for a victim and a perpetrator

- Asks "what, where, when, why, how" questions: What did you do, where, when, why?

A solution-focused approach pays less attention to why the problem developed, though that is still important. The *solution-focused approach*:

- Tries to increase times when there are no problems; looks for things going well

- Looks for a solution in which all involved can win

- Asks "when and how" questions: When will we stop this and start thinking about solving the problem? How can we find a solution that will prevent this problem from happening again?

When you use any intervention for bullies and victims together, it is essential to take a solution-focused approach. It is also critical that you support, not blame, the victim in any bully/victim interactions. (We will have more to say about supporting the victim in Module 5.)

Changing Behaviors

Through an open discussion with the bully and the victim, you can change behaviors:

1. Elicit suggestions from the bully and victim for targets of behavior change.

2. List and prioritize behaviors requiring change.

3. Construct a written contract; have both parties sign it.

4. Reward both bully and victim for improvements. Remember, change takes time. Be sure to reward for successive approximations to the desired behavior.

Altering Attitudes

Through an open discussion with the bully and the victim, you can alter attitudes:

1. Encourage the bully to identify and discuss the victim's behavior.

2. Encourage the victim to identify and discuss the bully's behavior.

3. Verify that the bully knows the effect his or her behavior is having on the victim.

4. Verify that the victim knows the effect his or her behavior is having on the bully.

5. Establish the reason(s) for the bullying/victimization:

    Is the bully compensating for some feeling of inadequacy?

    Is the bullying being carried out for fun and entertainment?

    Is the victim provoking the bully in an attempt to gain attention?

    Is the victim unknowingly provoking the bully?

6. Assist and encourage the bully and the victim to identify each other's strengths (e.g., skills, personality, etc.).

Using Collaborative Conflict Resolution

Collaborative conflict resolution (CCR) is an additional means of intervening in bullying situations. CCR is characterized by the opportunity for direct communication between disputants and gives disputants responsibility for finding their own solutions through negotiation (Cowie, 1994). When used with bullies and victims, an adult will need to facilitate the process. Basically, the steps toward a "win-win" outcome are as follows:

1. Identify wants and needs: State what you want and why you want it.

2. Listen: Listen carefully to what the other person says he or she wants and needs.

3. Brainstorm solutions: Think of all the ways you might solve the problem.

4. Choose a fair solution: Reconsider each idea and select solutions that will make everyone feel like a winner. If either the victim or the bully believes a solution is inequitable, you can be certain the problem will develop again. Both must agree that the solution is fair and reasonable.

5. Devise a plan of action: When you have agreed on a solution, plan how you will put it into action.

REPUTATION CHANGING

When students begin to change and behave more appropriately, there often is still a problem: Reputations do not change as fast as behavior can. Being violent and aggressive (i.e., a bully) results in a student's being rejected by classmates and shunned by others. Some teachers may also have this problem: Once a child has been labeled by the school as a bully or provocateur, he or she may be perceived that way long after the behavior has changed. Teachers will need to take an active role in helping other students recognize changes in and accept the former bully as a peer and fellow student. If students see a teacher modeling acceptance and social validation, they will model the teacher's behavior and begin to be more accepting as well.

In addition to modeling more accepting behavior, the teacher can actively incorporate the changed student into the group. That way peers can see the changes for themselves. Good forums for this are sports and recreational events, as well as class projects and assignments. Cooperative learning can help build cohesiveness among students and is a powerful way to incorporate the former bully into classroom group activities. These activities must be planned, though—they won't just happen.

CONTENT REVIEW

The following statements refer to the learning goals of this module. Take a minute to think about the statements. Ask yourself whether you feel confident that you can say yes to each. If not, please revisit those topics and consider ways to strengthen your learning.

I know that bullies are often hurt themselves and that they deserve help and support.   Yes ❑   No ❑

I understand the need for an "invitational approach" when working with bullies.   Yes ❑   No ❑

I recognize that bullying behavior serves a purpose and that bullies would often rather receive negative attention than none at all.   Yes ❑   No ❑

I have established classroom rules regarding bullying, and I am prepared to enforce them consistently and fairly.   Yes ❑   No ❑

I am committed to identifying and reinforcing positive behaviors in my classroom.   Yes ❑   No ❑

I understand the importance of intervening immediately in the bully-victim interaction to prevent harm as well as reinforcement the bully may receive from peers.   Yes ❑   No ❑

I am aware of my attitudes and responses toward victims and bullies so I do not accidentally reinforce inappropriate behaviors.   Yes ❑   No ❑

I am aware that bullies can benefit from direct instruction in several areas of development (e.g., problem solving, empathy).   Yes ❑   No ❑

I understand that becoming involved in more positive interactions with peers can help bullies change and that I can arrange opportunities for bullies to experience social success without aggression.   Yes ❑   No ❑

I realize it is difficult for bullies to change their reputation among their peers and that I can help classmates see changes in behavior.   Yes ❑   No ❑

A Reminder . . .

CLASSROOM INTERACTION AND AWARENESS CHART

Use the CIAC to describe any bullying behavior you observe (and that students report to you, if you wish). Specific instructions for filling out the CIAC appear in Appendix D, along with a blank copy of the chart.

THE BIG QUESTIONS

Focus yourself and honestly appraise your progress by asking yourself the "Big Questions." There are no right or wrong answers.

In relation to intervening with bullies in my school:

1. What is my goal?

2. What am I doing?

3. Is what I am doing helping me achieve my goal?

4. *(If not)* What can I do differently?

PERSONAL GOALS FORM

The Personal Goals Form, on the next page, is designed to help you tailor the content of this module to your own students and situation. If you have not filled out the form as you worked through the information component of the module, please take a moment to do so now.

Personal Goals Form

GOALS

- To learn the importance of an invitational approach in initiating contact and establishing rapport with bullies
- To learn the "Four R's" of bully control and some general strategies for intervening with bullies
- To understand basic behavior change principles as they relate to bullying
- To learn specific areas that can be developed in bullies to help them change their behaviors
- To learn interventions for bullies and victims together
- To understand how reputation plays a part in maintaining bullying behavior

1. My role in intervening in bullying incidents:

   _____

   _____

2. I have observed bullying incidents in my classroom that require intervention. *(Please record incidents on the Classroom Interaction and Awareness Chart. Under "Interventions," specify both your immediate response and an intervention you could use in the future.)*

3. I will conduct the following classroom activities to help my students continue to develop their awareness of bullying and their commitment to change.

   _____

   _____

4. I will evaluate the effectiveness of these activities by (a) recording incidents on the CIAC to see if there is a reduction across time, (b) monitoring the extent to which students report bullying situations, and (c) recording my impressions of change in the classroom environment. *(Please indicate any other means of evaluation in the space below.)*

   _____

   _____

5. I will give students feedback on their progress by (a) sharing the number and types of incidents recorded on the CIAC and (b) encouraging classroom discussion of these incidents and related issues. *(Please indicate any other means of feedback in the space below.)*

   _____

   _____

6. I will share my experiences in applying the information in this module with members of my Support Team, other teachers, administrators, parents. *(Please specify who and when in the space below.)*

   _____

   _____

Classroom Activities

STOP THE BULLYING

This activity requires a commitment from all of your students to take an active stand against bullying. Students develop a written agreement to work together in making your school a safe place for learning.

ANGER IS NORMAL

Often, when an event occurs, youths react impulsively. This activity will help youths identify problematic areas and how they respond to anger, both physically and cognitively. Discussion helps youths recognize their anger as well as discriminate healthy from unhealthy ways of dealing with anger.

CAGE YOUR LION

Most people do not know how to deal with anger. This activity provides a format for the open discussion of anger as a normal and common emotion that can and must be handled in a positive way.

FEEL THE HEAT

Anger causes a physiological response in various parts of the body. Students can become aware of what is happening in their bodies when they are becoming angry and can learn to recognize early warning signs that they or their peers may lose control and act irresponsibly. Better awareness means more time for youth to cope with their anger before responding.

Stop the Bullying

GOALS

- To encourage students to agree to take an active role in preventing bullying

- To allow students to express their thoughts and ideas on how to prevent bully/victim interactions

- To encourage students to support one another in their efforts to deal with bullying

MATERIALS

- Stop the Bullying worksheet

DIRECTIONS

1. Distribute copies of the Stop the Bullying worksheet, one per student.

2. Ask students to address, in writing: (a) What they plan to do to prevent bullying and (b) How and in what ways they plan on achieving support from fellow classmates. Point out that dwelling on problems often distracts us from finding solutions, and help students develop solution-oriented approaches (as discussed in the introduction to this book).

3. Have students discuss with the class the steps they plan to take to help prevent bullying. As they discuss the points, raise the following questions:

   - What will you need to make this happen?

   - What changes do you need to make for this to happen?

   - What might go wrong with the plan? What might you do if this happens? (In this way you encourage students to engage in "pre–problem solving"—anticipating ways to deal with problems before they happen.)

   As students discuss their plans, emphasize the role of friends, fellow students, and other peers in helping to carry out their plans. Ask questions such as the following:

   - With whom will you do this?

- How will these people help?

- What will you do if these people are not available?

- Who else might work with you?

- Are there adults who might also become involved with your plan?

4. Process the activity by conducting a class discussion.

DISCUSSION

1. What are some solutions you will use to stop bullying?

2. What could go wrong with your plan—that is, what incidents/events would make it difficult to carry out your plan?

3. What can you do to plan ahead for these incidents/events? Who could help you stick to your plan?

4. What can you do to help others stick to their pledge to "Stop the Bullying"? Keep your pledge?

5. How do you feel when you keep your pledge?

6. How do you feel when you fail to keep your pledge?

NOTE

It is important to review students' plans to be certain they are not setting highly unrealistic goals or putting themselves in the way of harm. Whereas most students develop very reasonable plans, some students' plans involve coercion and aggression, the very behaviors that we hope to reduce.

STOP THE BULLYING

I pledge to actively make my school a safer place
for all students. I promise I will do the following
to stop the bullying:

_____

_____

_____

_____

_____

_____

To achieve my goal, I will need support
from my classmates in the following ways:

_____

_____

_____

_____

_____

Signed: _____

Anger Is Normal

OBJECTIVES

- To help students understand that anger is a normal part of life
- To generate a list of anger-provoking situations
- To recognize stimuli that lead to anger
- To illustrate the range of healthy and unhealthy ways to express anger

MATERIALS

- Chalkboard or easel pad

DIRECTIONS

1. On the chalkboard or easel pad, write the statement "What makes you angry?"

2. Ask students to brainstorm situations that provoke anger.

3. Record student responses on the chalkboard or easel pad. If students are silent, prompt them with questions like the following:

   - What about school makes you angry?
   - What about your family makes you angry?
   - What do your friends do that makes you angry?

4. Discuss the anger list with students, emphasizing the multiple causes of anger. Explain that everyone feels angry at some point and that what one chooses to do about that feeling can be healthy or unhealthy.

5. Divide the chalkboard or easel pad into two columns: "Healthy Ways to Express Anger" and "Unhealthy Ways to Express Anger."

6. Ask the students to brainstorm the ways that they deal with anger and to categorize each as either healthy or unhealthy. (Depending on your group, you may wish to use the terms *functional anger* and *dysfunctional anger.*) If necessary, prompt students with questions like the following:

   - How do you deal with anger?
   - What do you do when you become angry?
   - What are some ways you have seen others deal with anger?

7. Record students' responses in the respective columns. Under "Healthy Ways to Express Anger" students may suggest thinking calming thoughts, walking away, talking the problem out with the person, going to a teacher or another adult for help, or blowing off steam by exercising or playing a sport. Under "Unhealthy Ways to Express Anger," students may name reactions such as having a tantrum, hitting someone, yelling, or spreading rumors or otherwise trying to get revenge. When finished, ask whether students would make any changes to the list and what criteria they used to categorize each way of dealing with anger.

8. Process the activity by conducting a class discussion.

DISCUSSION

- Why is the idea that you have to "act out" your anger erroneous?

- What do you think of the idea that you can choose how you respond if you are feeling angry?

- Can you think of people who have good control of their angry feelings? How do you think they stay in charge?

- The next time you feel angry, what do you think you might try instead of losing control?

NOTE

Some students may find the idea of choosing a response to an angering situation quite surprising. The point to emphasize in this activity is that alternatives do exist and that if a person is in charge of himself or herself, there is never a reason to act out aggressively.

Cage Your Lion

OBJECTIVES

- To help students become aware of and recognize behaviors that make them angry

- To allow students to explore positive alternatives to handling their anger

MATERIALS

- Cage Your Lion worksheet

DIRECTIONS

1. Distribute the Cage Your Lion worksheet, one per student. Ask the class to complete it.

2. When students have finished, discuss the first three questions. Discuss the idea that everyone gets angry—it is even good to express anger, otherwise it can build up to a point where we may hurt others or maybe even get sick ourselves. What is important is that people learn how to control their anger so it does not control them.

3. Next discuss the fourth question, concerning positive alternatives to behaving in an aggressive way. Stress that alternatives to acting out anger exist and that students are responsible for making their own choices and taking charge of their own lives.

4. Conduct a class discussion, using the following questions.

DISCUSSION

- How does it feel to talk about situations in which you feel angry?

- Do people in the class get angry about the same or different kinds of situations? What are some examples?

- Does everyone do the same thing when he or she feels angry? Feel the same thing? What are some examples?

- What were some ways people wanted to change in the situations they identified? Do you think these ways might work?

NOTE

One effective way to illustrate that students do in fact have a choice in how they respond in emotional situations is to have them consider the message commonly conveyed in the media, particularly song lyrics, that they do not have such control. Invite students to ask themselves why the media would portray adolescents as out of control and unable to behave responsibly. Students can identify lyrics they have heard, then discuss how they can exert control.

Cage Your Lion

1   What makes me really upset is when . . .

2   When I get upset in this situation, I usually . . .

3   After I get upset, I feel . . .

4   A better way of handling the situation would
    be to . . .

Feel the Heat

OBJECTIVES

- To help students recognize the physiological changes that occur with anger

- To aid students in accepting anger as a part of life

MATERIALS

- Feel the Heat worksheet

DIRECTIONS

1. Give each student a Feel the Heat worksheet.

2. Ask students to think about the physical changes that take place in their bodies when they begin to get angry—for instance, "My heart starts to beat really fast."

3. Ask students to draw arrows to the parts of the body affected by their anger (e.g., "Draw an arrow to your heart if you feel it begins to race when you are angry").

4. Conduct a class discussion, using the following questions.

DISCUSSION

- How does anger begin?

- What causes anger?

- What causes us to feel anger in our bodies?

- Do we have control over whether or not we want to feel the anger in our bodies?

- Do different types of situations cause different types of anger? If so, do you feel the anger in different places in your body?

- How are the feelings in your body resulting from anger different from feelings that come from other emotions (fear, love, and so on)? Are there any similarities?

FEEL THE HEAT

Instructions: Think about the physical changes you notice in your body when you begin to get angry. On the figure below, draw an arrow to the parts of your body that are affected by your anger. For example, you would draw an arrow to your heart if you feel it begins to race when you are angry.

Module 4: Taking Charge—Interventions for Bullying Behavior

MODULE

5 Assisting Victims: Recommendations and Interventions

GOALS

- To become aware of the need for victim support

- To learn general strategies for intervening with victims

- To understand ways victims may change to avoid being targets for victimization

- To learn specific interventions helpful with passive, provocative, and bystander victims

- To learn the importance of assimilating victims into the class

OVERVIEW

In Module 3, we described who the victims are and what circumstances result in their being victimized. Understanding why, though, doesn't provide the "how," which is the purpose of this module. With attention commonly focused on bullies and bullying behaviors, the needs of victims are often neglected. Victims need to know they are not alone. Teachers can help in many ways—from establishing an open-door policy to helping victims avoid being targets for bullying to assimilating such students into the class. Once teachers are aware of what is maintaining victimization, they can become powerful catalysts for change.

VICTIM SUPPORT

At 25, I still can't stand the thought of the kids who picked on me. They locked me in a closet, took my money, made fun of me. . . . It's 12 years later—I think of it and I am filled with rage.

—25-year-old man

Being a victim of bullying is terrifying. It is sad but true that victims often have nobody to whom they may turn for support. Often, they fear that seeking help will cause the bullying to escalate, or in the past they have witnessed teachers neglecting to help other victims or been denied help themselves. Victims need to know that they are not in this alone and that they can seek support from teachers to help them cope with the situation and develop solutions to reduce and eliminate victimization.

Richard Hazler (1996) has identified the following times it is appropriate for victims to seek assistance from teachers or other school personnel:

1. Any time a student is uncomfortable with a situation is a good time to seek support in evaluating the situation and looking for productive solutions. Example: "Ms. Smith, Maria and her friends hang out in the girls' bathroom. Every time I go to use the bathroom they give me 'the look.' They haven't done anything to me, but I'm scared to go back in there."

2. When the victim is in danger of being physically or emotionally harmed, adult intervention should be sought immediately. Example: "Ms. Smith, Lucas is really mad at me and said he was going to hurt me after school. He said he has a knife and is going to cut me. I don't know what to do."

3. When a bullying situation continues even though the student has worked with others to solve the problem, adult intervention should be sought. Example: "Ms. Smith, I know we have talked about this before and I have tried to do the things we talked about, but Joanne is still knocking my books over in the hallway and threatening me on the school bus."

GENERAL STRATEGIES FOR INTERVENING WITH VICTIMS

The following strategies are useful for intervening with victims, in either the classroom or larger school environment.

Create an open-door policy

Let students know that your door is always open and that they can seek your support at all times in a caring, nonjudgmental atmosphere. Encourage them to ask for your help before they are in immediate danger of being bullied.

Respond to reports of minor incidents

In a workshop we were conducting, a teacher asked an important question: "What about the student who consistently seeks you out to tattle on classmates?" Teachers express great frustration with this type of situation and may ignore the student who complains because they feel students need to learn how to solve problems on their own. You can use these small incidents as a training ground for larger ones. Let the complainer know you care, but educate him or her to evaluate the seriousness of the situation and think of productive solutions. If children receive support for minor incidents from teachers, then they will be more likely to seek support for major occurrences.

Take the incident or report seriously

One of the biggest fears victims have is that, in addition to being victimized by a bully, they will also be laughed at or ignored by the teacher. Feelings are not right or wrong—they just are. Reassure the victim, and make every attempt to avoid making the victim feel inadequate or foolish. If you are nonempathic and discount a victim's concerns, you are, in effect, revictimizing the student. Even when you may not be able to do anything to alleviate the problem, the act of listening to the victim and giving your assurance that you understand and will help work on the problem is supportive and positive.

Take action with the bully as soon as possible

Share your disapproval with the bully right away—the longer the bully goes on believing that he or she will not be reprimanded or corrected, the more firmly entrenched the belief that he or she was right and "got away with it" will be. During the confrontation, encourage the bully to try to understand the victim's view of the problem—in other words, use the experience to help the bully become more empathic. A frank discussion of the bullying event (identifying the problem behavior), the impact on the victim (empathy training), and what steps must be taken (providing appropriate consequences) will help the bully stop and think before engaging in that behavior again. Punish the bully if necessary. If you do, clearly explain the punishment and why it is being given.

Offer concrete help, advice, and support to the victim

The victim will benefit if you take the situation seriously, become involved quickly with the bully, provide a consequence to the bully to discourage reoccurence of the behavior, then offer specific help to the victim. The specific help should focus on the conflict: what happened, whether there was a way to see the situation coming, and what steps could have reduced the seriousness of the incident. Support, recommendations for prevention, and a plan for doing things differently in the future can be very empowering.

Provide follow-up support for the victim

After you have intervened in a bullying situation, it is important to follow through. Immediately following the incident, we recommend that you check in with the victim on a daily basis until it is clear that the victim is no longer being victimized. Remind the victim that he or she is always free to discuss the problem and that all discussions will be confidential. You might say, for example, "Lee, my door is always open to you. When we talk I won't be sharing the discussion with any of the other students. Anything that you say about troubles with other students will be kept between you and me as long as we can handle the situation without you or others suffering harm. Feel free to stop by any time."

TEACHING VICTIMS TO CHANGE THEIR BEHAVIORS

There's one kid—he's just annoying. . . . I just want to say, "Shut up—get out of my face." If I were a teacher I'd like to kick him out the door before he set foot in my classroom and say, "Boy, what are you thinking? Get out!"

—14-year-old boy

Behaviors performed by victims stimulate responses from bullies. If victims can learn to alter their behaviors, this in turn will affect bullies' response, potentially decreasing or eliminating the bullying over time. We want to stress that by suggesting this approach, we are not implying that the responsibility for change rests solely with victims. We don't want to strip victims of their identity by teaching them to behave differently. Instead, when we engage victims in this kind of teaching, we explore with students the changes they may be interested in and willing to make.

Obviously, some characteristics cannot be changed—for example, one's height or ethnic background. We invite students to look at voluntary social behaviors and activities that elicit the attention of bullies. There is distinction between "blaming the victim" and giving a student access to instruction that he or she chooses and feels will be personally useful. No student should live in fear and anxiety, so at the same time we offer help of this sort, we work to encourage other students to be more accepting of individual differences.

It is a good idea to identify victims in your class as early as possible and to meet with them individually to discuss their desire to learn these and other ways to decrease their victimization. To preserve and, we would hope, enhance these students' self-concept, any work along these lines you mutually agree to undertake should highlight strengths as well as address weaknesses.

Nonvictim Responses

Hazler (1996) has identified four changes victims can make to help reduce or eliminate their victimization.

Avoid giving the bully an emotional payoff

The more intensely the victim reacts in a way the bully wants, the greater the bully's pleasure. When victims find ways to rob the bully of an emotional payoff, this reduces the bully's pleasure and makes them much less desirable targets.

> *Harry is a bully. His target for the last several months has been a bright girl named Raquel in his math class. He calls her "chubs to the fifth power." Raquel used to get tears in her eyes and slouch down in her chair in shame. With her teacher's help Raquel learned how to grin and walk away when Harry teases her. Harry has since given up trying to harass Raquel.*

Be physically and verbally assertive, not aggressive

Bullies seek targets who shy away from standing up for themselves. When victims use assertive words and behaviors, they communicate that they know their rights. Victims can convey confidence simply by altering their body language—standing up straight rather than slouching and making eye contact rather than looking away.

> *No one picks on Raymond. He's cool and confident. However, Willy is every bully's target. One day Willy decided to try Raymond's slick moves. He stood up tall and told his tormentor, "Get a life!" His tormentor didn't mess with him again!*

Do something unexpected

Predictability of response increases the likelihood that the bully will continue to harass a particular person. Victims can decrease the chance that they will be bullied by making their reactions less predictable.

When victims respond in an inconsistent manner (e.g., walking away when before they burst into tears) or with distracting behaviors (e.g., talking loudly), this leaves the bully uncertain as to what will happen next. Their unpredictability makes them less attractive targets

> *Every time Tina bullied Deja, Deja would cower in the corner and begin to tremble. Tina loved this and continued to feel powerful over Deja. One day, Deja didn't hide in the corner. Instead, she told Tina to get lost, then walked over and joined a group of students at the lunch table.*

Strengthen existing friendships and make new ones

Victims are often selected because they have few friends or friends who are not willing to stand by them in difficult times. Strengthening existing friendships and developing new ones are among the best methods for reversing the trend of "victim isolation." There is safety in numbers: When victims are in an accepting crowd, this makes them less desirable targets. Victims should seek ways to be with their friends at times they are generally harassed.

> *Vic moved to a new school in the seventh grade. Being new, he was not included in any of the regular groups around school. He was not invited to sit at lunch with anyone. He was small, and before long he began to attract the attention of one of the neighborhood bullies. Vic joined a YMCA in town and took classes in karate and tai chi. He began to develop confidence from his activities, and he used his experiences to make new friends, both at the YMCA and with people at school who had seen him there. Other students were interested in martial arts training, and Vic was accepted into several groups at school. The bully stopped hanging around.*

Social Skills

Victims often lack the social skills they need for peer interaction. Fortunately, such skills can be taught and learned (Goldstein & McGinnis, 1997; McGinnis & Goldstein, 1997). The steps in social skills training are enumerated in Module 4. For victims, instruction in the following areas can be especially helpful:

- Self-presentation skills (e.g., eye contact, posture, facial expressions)

- Conflict resolution skills

- Assertiveness skills

- Interpersonal skills (e.g., teamwork, cooperation)

Social skills instruction can take place in a variety of settings and in a number of ways. If you have established a safe, supportive classroom atmosphere, you may want to teach these types of skills to everyone in the class. Victims know who they are, and it is likely that all of the other students also know who has been victimized. The whole-class approach emphasizes the importance of having all present be responsible for helping address the problem. In addition, using the whole class as a skill-building, solution-seeking group can provide enormous emotional support and validation for victims. The approach also may allow students who have been bystanders when bullying occurred to take a more active role in identifying what stopped them from responding. One effective classroom method involves the use of a video camera. Students may be videotaped trying various roles and demonstrating various behaviors that are of concern. Observing videotapes is an excellent way of "seeing ourselves as others see us" and provides the opportunity for identifying changes we wish to make.

Social skills can also be taught to students in small groups. Often, a member of the school counseling staff has expertise in social skills instruction and will conduct such groups. Social skills may be taught to individual students, but because the skills to be learned are interpersonal in nature, individual instruction is less desirable than small-group instruction.

INTERVENTIONS FOR SPECIFIC TYPES OF VICTIMS

In Module 3, we discussed the different types of victims—passive, provocative, and bystander—noting that each group has particular difficulties and needs. Passive victims are the most commonly targeted. They tend to be very anxious and insecure, and to react to bullying with fear and frustration. Provocative victims are distinguished from passive victims by the fact that they are, like bullies, aggressive. These youth tend to provoke others deliberately for the attention it gains them. Bystander victims are youth indirectly affected by bullying. They often feel guilty and weak because they do not stand up to bullies or report bullying incidents. They also tend to live in fear of becoming the direct target of bullying.

Passive Victims

The main focus of interventions for passive victims is providing adequate social support. You may not be readily accessible at the time or place bullying occurs, but other members of your Support Team may be, and they will have the knowledge and skills necessary to provide this kind of help. One job of the Support Team, then, should be to help one another's students when problems arise. The Support Team can also develop specific skills and interventions that incorporate helping and understanding victims; these materials could be shared in the classes of each participating teacher.

Establish a victims anonymous group

A victims anonymous group is a student-based group that serves as a safe haven in which victims can report bullying incidents and seek support. Some schools have supported the establishment of such a group with the intention of its becoming a vehicle for problem solving as well as support. When it comes to generating solutions, it is certainly true that "the whole is greater than the sum of its parts." The focus on support and mutual understanding must be maintained, even if part of the group's goal is to look for ways to reduce victimization in the school.

Identify the behaviors or characteristics of the victim that elicit the bullying acts and assist in facilitating necessary changes

As we discussed earlier, victims may be able to change behaviors and characteristics that evoke bullying, if they so choose. Both passive and provocative victims may benefit from this approach. Talking about and attempting to change behaviors that have resulted in a victim's being targeted is controversial: Students do not want to be blamed for being victimized, and there is a chance that even if a student changes an identified behavior, the bullying may continue. If the change does not help, the victim may become more vulnerable and less optimistic.

Assist the victim in building confidence and self-esteem

Bullies tend to seek targets who lack confidence and shy away from standing up for themselves. You can assist passive victims in building self-confidence by helping them enhance social and problem-solving skills, as well as by highlighting their strengths. If passive victims can bolster their self-concept, they will be less likely to submit to bullying.

Provocative Victims

Provocative victims instigate aggression in others and are victimized in the process because they often are smaller and less competent than the person provoked. This behavior may occur for a number of reasons, as described in Module 3. Because these victims are also provocateurs, it is important to help them learn how to avoid instigating aggression. This is the main focus for this type of victim. Some specific suggestions follow:

- Assist provocative victims in gaining insight into their perceptions of the bully. Start by having victims describe the characteristics that draw them to instigate trouble with the bully (e.g., they enjoy the attention, think it is funny, think the other person deserves it).

- Help victims identify the consequences of provoking the bully. Have victims make a list or talk about the results of provoking the bully (e.g., they are pushed or shoved, verbally abused, mocked by other students in the school).

- Help victims weigh the costs and benefits of these consequences.

- Help victims make desired changes. Assist them in developing alternative prosocial behaviors.

Taking provocative victims through the Big Questions helps them clarify their goals (e.g., to get along with others, not to be hurt and/or victimized by others), understand their role in the bullying, and develop plans for change. Clearly, provocation is not helping these victims achieve their goals. With this understanding, these victims may be more willing to develop alternative behaviors. Again, the Big Questions are as follows:

1. What is my goal?

2. What am I doing?

3. Is what I am doing helping me to achieve my goal?

4. *(If not)* What can I do differently?

The following dialogue illustrates how one teacher applied these questions after witnessing a student being pushed and shoved in the recreation area.

Teacher: Patrick, I'm bringing you back to the classroom so you can get cooled down. On the one hand, it looks like you are the victim of some heavy-duty aggression, yet as I watched the incident develop, it seems the other students were talking and playing a game, and you barged in. When they said they didn't want you to participate, you got angry and belligerent. Then they got up and started hitting on you. They shouldn't do that, and I'm meeting with them in a few minutes, but in the meantime, what is going on with you?

Patrick: Nothing.

Teacher: It seems you had a goal of being involved with the group, but when you tried to join in, you ended up in a fight.

Patrick: It isn't my fault. All I wanted to do was join their game.

Teacher: So your goal is to be able to join others in their games?

Patrick: Yes.

Teacher: What you attempted to do was force your way in. Did it work?

Patrick: No.

Teacher: Then what can you do differently?

Patrick: I don't know.

Teacher: Let's spend a few minutes thinking, exploring what else you could do.

The teacher then discussed skills Patrick could work on to help him become more adept at joining groups. Patrick and the teacher also talked about whether the group in question is an appropriate group for him to try to join. It is not the teacher's job to force a group of kids into accepting someone. Friendships can't be forced, but they can be facilitated.

Bystander Victims

Observers of bullying and victimization often receive little attention. Their confused feelings and concerns also will need to be addressed. Hazler (1996) has identified several techniques to assist bystander victims.

Help bystanders recognize their feelings and the fact that they are not alone in these feelings

Bystanders want things to be different and desire to help; however, they are afraid of being physically or emotionally hurt if they get involved. The fear that comes with observing an aggressive act is rarely discussed openly. More often, students walk away and remain silent. They do not want to admit that they felt intimidated or failed to step forward to help. Sometimes these feelings are referred to as "survivor guilt" or "survivor trauma," the feelings of guilt one develops for having survived a traumatic situation when others experienced more pain and suffering. It is important to discuss these feelings and to let bystanders know that others share their experience. This helps alleviate the feeling of victim isolation.

Encourage bystanders to get involved as a group rather than remain in isolation

Talking about their emotional experiences can help bystanders normalize their feelings of guilt and fear. At the same time, it may motivate them to become more active in working to reduce bullying. By knowing others are with them—feeling that "We're all in this together"—students are empowered to take on the injustices they encounter.

Bystanders can help victims in one of two ways: through direct intervention or through personal support. *Direct intervention* might take the form of a group of students intervening in the immediate conflict situation to confront the bully and protect the victim. The larger the number of bystanders, the greater the likelihood for successful direct intervention. Any efforts to intervene directly should be made cautiously, preferably in consultation with the teacher or another member of the school staff. *Personal support* might take the form of being available to and understanding of the victim. Bystanders might spend time with the victim, invite the victim to get involved in group activities, encourage the victim's efforts and accomplishments, and find ways to be good listeners. While remaining anonymous to the bully, students can let the victim know they are concerned. They can also help indirectly by not reinforcing the bully with laughter or verbal encouragement or repeating malicious rumors.

Train bystanders in peer mediation

Peer mediation programs offer a way for students to work together to resolve conflict in a peaceful way. In peer mediation, students are trained to maintain confidentiality, listen objectively, and help disputing parties work through the following procedures to find mutually agreeable solutions:

1. Agree to mediate

2. Gather points of view

3. Focus on interests

4. Create win-win options

5. Evaluate options

6. Create an agreement

A good resource for developing a peer mediation program—and the one from which these steps are drawn—is *Peer Mediation: Conflict Resolution in Schools* (Schrumpf, Crawford, & Bodine, 1997). Bystanders can benefit greatly by becoming involved in such programs: Knowing there is a peaceful way to resolve conflict is empowering, as is knowing one can play an active role in helping others solve problems.

ASSIMILATING VICTIMS INTO THE GROUP

At the beginning of the year I let my students know that I arrive to school 20 minutes before my classroom's homeroom and at the end of the day, I am in my classroom for 30 minutes after the bell rings. I tell them if they need to talk to me, I am here.

—Seventh-grade teacher

Reducing the bullying and victimization of particular students is only half the job. The other half is helping these students become a part of the class, assimilating them into the life of the group. Once labeled "victim," it may be quite difficult for a child to be accepted by the group (Besag, 1989). On the other hand, as adults we can point out in many ways that the victim is someone unfairly targeted by the bully. Recognizing that we are all vulnerable and that no one deserves to be victimized is an important step in understanding that all people are potential victims and that only by supporting everyone can we prevent ourselves from becoming targeted for mistreatment. By encouraging members of the class to develop stronger empathy for those less skilled or less protected, we can help both former and present victims become a more accepted part of the classroom group.

In assimilating victims, it is essential to assess the full context of the situation. Some victims may be resistant to shedding their established role because they experience secondary gains, perhaps receiving support and sympathy from classmates as a result of being persecuted. It may be that parents attend to them only when they are targeted by a troublemaker. Finally, some students' perceptions of themselves as victims are so deeply ingrained that to change they may need the assistance of a mental health professional.

As teachers, we must ask what the victim's status will be once the bullying has stopped. Will the victim just be ignored, lost in the crowd? Some students have recognition when they are bullied but have no role in a class when they are no longer the target of contempt. It is important to make sure that all students have a role in the class, that all are recognized and incorporated into the general makeup of the group. Each student should feel noticed and important each day, and when a student has a history of being targeted for aggression, that student may need more than the usual attention.

As we have discussed, there are many ways to help students who are bullied become accepted and supported. By implementing the program described in this manual, we are moving toward a more supportive and understanding environment, in which we think of students not as victims but as classmates and peers.

CONTENT REVIEW

The following statements refer to the learning goals of this module. Take a minute to think about the statements. Ask yourself whether you feel confident that you can say yes to each. If not, please revisit those topics and consider ways to strengthen your learning.

I have an open-door policy in my classroom that allows students to come to me for help against bullying.	Yes ❏	No ❏
I have communicated to my students that I would like them to ask me for my help immediately rather than wait until they are in immediate danger of being bullied.	Yes ❏	No ❏
I know that it is appropriate for a student to seek help when that student feels uncomfortable, when the victimization escalates from verbal to physical abuse, and when bullying persists even after a teacher has been informed.	Yes ❏	No ❏
I understand the role of the victim in the bully/victim interaction and feel confident that I can help the victim alter his or her role.	Yes ❏	No ❏
I am able to identify and highlight victims' strengths to help them achieve a more positive self-concept.	Yes ❏	No ❏
I know that by teaching social skills, I can help students improve their interpersonal relations and become less desirable targets for bullying.	Yes ❏	No ❏
I feel competent in addressing the needs of different types of victims: passive, provocative, and bystander.	Yes ❏	No ❏
I know that a victims anonymous group can have a positive impact on victims' sense of control over their own lives and ability to deal with bullying incidents.	Yes ❏	No ❏
I am aware that peer mediation is an effective strategy to help students resolve conflicts in a peaceful way.	Yes ❏	No ❏

A Reminder . . .

CLASSROOM INTERACTION AND AWARENESS CHART

Use the CIAC to describe any bullying behavior you observe (and that students report to you, if you wish). Specific instructions for filling out the CIAC appear in Appendix D, along with a blank copy of the chart.

THE BIG QUESTIONS

Focus yourself and honestly appraise your progress by asking yourself the "Big Questions." There are no right or wrong answers.

With regard to helping victims:

1. What is my goal?

2. What am I doing?

3. Is what I am doing helping me achieve my goal?

4. *(If not)* What can I do differently?

PERSONAL GOALS FORM

The Personal Goals Form, on the next page, is designed to help you tailor the content of this module to your own students and situation. If you have not filled out the form as you worked through the information component of the module, please take a moment to do so now.

Personal Goals Form

GOALS

- To become aware of the need for victim support

- To learn general strategies for intervening with victims

- To understand ways victims may change to avoid being targets for victimization

- To learn specific interventions helpful with passive, provocative, and bystander victims

- To learn the importance of assimilating victims into the class

1. My role in assisting victims:

   _____

   _____

2. I have observed incidents of victimization in my classroom. *(Please record incidents on the Classroom Interaction and Awareness Chart. Under "Interventions," specify both your immediate response and a way you could support the victim.)*

3. I will conduct the following classroom activities to help my students continue to develop their awareness of victimization and their commitment to change.

   _____

   _____

4. I will evaluate the effectiveness of these activities by (a) recording incidents on the CIAC to see if there is a reduction across time, (b) monitoring the extent to which students report bullying situations, and (c) recording my impressions of change in the classroom environment. *(Please indicate any other means of evaluation in the space below.)*

   _____

   _____

5. I will give students feedback on their progress by (a) sharing the number and types of incidents recorded on the CIAC and (b) encouraging classroom discussion of these incidents and related issues. *(Please indicate any other means of feedback in the space below.)*

   _____

   _____

6. I will share my experiences in applying the information in this module with members of my Support Team, other teachers, administrators, parents. *(Please specify who and when in the space below.)*

   _____

   _____

Classroom Activities

ARE YOU UP FOR THE CHALLENGE?

This activity helps conquer rumors. Together, students recognize rumors and their own role in spreading them. They take on the challenge of preventing rumor spreading and verbal victimization.

STRENGTH-O-METER

Students often do not recognize the power individuals need to stand up for themselves. This activity helps students recognize their personal strength and the amount of help they need from others to deal with difficult situations. Together, students discuss their ability to recognize when they and their peers need help in fighting the "bullies battle." Through this activity, they become prepared to ask for support and to give appropriate support to others.

A PIECE OF THE PIE

Victimization often occurs to individuals who have difficulty with social skills. This exercise helps students perfect the skill of becoming a part of the group. The class can discuss the challenges of entering a group as well as become more empathic toward students who find this skill difficult.

GOING FOR THE GOLD

Students often know what others do not like about them but seldom know what characteristics others value. This activity provides an opportunity for classmates to share the positive qualities and strengths they see in one another. Students typically find this activity extremely valuable and tend to remember their classmates' compliments long after the activity is over.

Are You Up for the Challenge?

OBJECTIVES

- To assist students in recognizing how rumors are spread and how these rumors affect the individuals involved

- To help students understand their responsibility in disrupting the "rumor chain"

MATERIALS

- None

DIRECTIONS

1. Read the following scenario aloud to the class, then discuss:

   Cathy told Linda that her friend Mary was telling other classmates that Linda received the lowest grade on the science test and was obviously the dumbest girl in the class. Linda was so upset that Mary would spread such a horrible rumor that she thought she would really get back at Mary. So Linda decided to tell Cathy a deep secret that Mary had confided in her about a family problem. Cathy began sharing Mary's secret with her classmates. When Mary overheard her classmates laughing about her family's problem, she was crushed and refused to return to school the next day. Later, Linda found out that Mary had never said anything about her—rather, Cathy was spreading rumors.

2. Challenge students: "For one day, you can say only positive things about your classmates. It may be tough . . . are you up for the challenge?"

3. Process the activity by conducting a class discussion.

DISCUSSION

- Have rumors been spread about you? How did you feel?

- Have you and your friends spread rumors about your classmates?

- Have you ever taken the responsibility to stop a rumor from being spread?

- How would it feel to know that classmates will not talk negatively about you?

- Can you imagine having only positive comments made about you?

Strength-o-Meter

OBJECTIVES

- To help students understand others' need for support when they are being victimized

- To assist students in recognizing the amount of strength required to endure bullying

- To encourage students to ask for help when it is necessary

MATERIALS

- Strength-o-Meter worksheet

DIRECTIONS

1. Give one copy of the Strength-o-Meter worksheet to each student.

2. Ask students to read the scenarios and respond to each one by coloring in the thermometer to represent the degree to which they can handle the situation by themselves and the degree to which they need help from others.

3. Process the activity by conducting a class discussion about how students marked the thermometers.

DISCUSSION

- Are there particular bullying situations in which you need additional help? Which ones?

- From whom may you seek help when handling a difficult situation?

- Are there times you can handle situations by yourself? How do these situations differ from those in which you feel you need to ask for help?

- Do you find it difficult to ask others for help?

- Do you usually receive help when you request it from others?

- How do you feel when you ask for help? Weak? Insecure? Anxious? Confident? Strong?

STRENGTH-O-METER

Instructions: Read each of the following scenarios. Respond to each by coloring in the thermometer to represent how much you can handle by yourself and how much help you need from others.

I can handle this much by myself.   **I need this much help from others.**

1 You are being tormented in the lunchroom. One kid tripped you, but luckily you did not drop your tray. As soon as you sit down, another student comes by and swipes your sandwich.

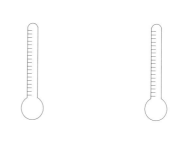

2 As soon as you get on the bus and take your seat, the kids behind you start blowing spitballs in your hair and calling you names.

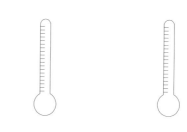

3 In gym class, you are getting ready to play kickball. As always, you are the last one to be chosen for a team. When the teacher assigns you to a team, everyone begins to complain.

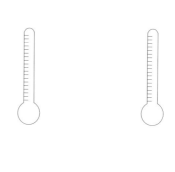

4 You are in history class. The teacher asks a question. You know the answer, and you quickly raise your hand. Your response is followed by giggles and whispers from the class.

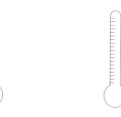

A Piece of the Pie

OBJECTIVES

- To assist students in feeling more comfortable entering a group

- To help members of a group to recognize when someone is attempting to become part of the group

- To build group-entry skills and confidence in group settings

MATERIALS

- Chalkboard or easel pad

DIRECTIONS

1. Brainstorm ways that a person can enter a group in the following settings:

   Lunchroom

   Hallway

   Playground

   Gym class

2. Write the various suggestions on the chalkboard or easel pad.

3. Divide the class into groups of four. Ask three group members to engage in a conversation while the fourth practices entering the group. Allow each group member an opportunity to enter the group. Instruct group members to be receptive and welcoming to the entering group member.

4. Process the activity by conducting a class discussion.

DISCUSSION

- How did you feel right before you attempted to enter the group?

- Were there differences in class members' attempts to enter the group? If so, what were these?

- Did the group readily accept your entrance?

- What thoughts and feelings did you experience when you attempted to enter the group?

- How would it feel if the group did not pay attention to you when you tried to join them?

- Can you think of a time this may have happened to you? What could you have done differently?

Going for the Gold

OBJECTIVES

- To assist students in becoming aware of their strengths
- To assist students in experiencing the feeling of being valued and appreciated
- To help class members look for the positive qualities in their peers
- To assist students who view themselves in a negative manner to view themselves more positively

MATERIALS

- Index cards (enough so each student has one for every other student in the class)

DIRECTIONS

1. Explain that every individual has positive qualities. It is easy to see the qualities you like in your friends, but it can be more difficult to see the strengths in people you know less well.

2. Hand out the index cards, then instruct each student to write every other student's name on the front of a separate index card. On the back of each card, students write two positive qualities about the student named. For example:

   I like your strength.

   You speak well in class.

   You are a true friend.

   You are a hard worker.

3. Collect the cards and screen them for appropriateness, then give each student the cards on which his or her name is written. Tell students to keep the cards. If they are feeling down or need a boost, they can read them and remind themselves of all of their great qualities.

4. Conduct a class discussion, using the following questions.

DISCUSSION

- How did it feel to write down the positive characteristics of your classmates?

- How did it feel to get cards back with your positive attributes?

- Are there other items you are proud of or happy about that your classmates may have missed? If so, please write them on a card and add to your collection.

MODULE

6 The Role of Prevention

OVERVIEW

The modules preceding this one have focused on understanding and identifying the bullies and victims among us, as well as on the development of interventions appropriate for teachers to use with bullies and victims. Although it is essential that we understand and intervene with bullies and victims, it is perhaps even more important to prevent bullying and victimization from occurring in the first place. To repeat the lifeguard analogy from the introduction of this manual: It is important to save the lives of swimmers who are in trouble in the water, but it is also vital to teach swimming skills so we need fewer lifeguards. In other words, we must work with our students to develop prevention and early intervention plans so we have fewer bullying incidents with which to contend.

GOALS

- To understand the need for and basic principles of prevention

- To become aware of school characteristics that affect bullying

- To become aware of teacher characteristics that influence bullying

- To learn specific "hands-on" ways to prevent bullying and victimization in the classroom

PREVENTION ISSUES

Primary prevention has been defined as "An intervention intentionally designed to reduce the future incidence of adjustment problems in currently normal populations as well as efforts directed at the promotion of mental health functioning" (Durlak & Wells, 1997, p. 117). The goal of primary prevention is to forestall problems of adaptation and prevent dysfunction (Coie, Dodge, & Coppotelli, 1982). Lewis and Lewis (1983) indicate that prevention assumes that "equipping people with personal and environmental resources for coping is the best of all ways to ward off maladaptive problems, not trying to deal (however skillfully) with problems that have already germinated and flowered" (p. 6). Conyne (1987) asserts that primary prevention focuses on collaboration and empowerment, rather than on individual remediation, and that the target of the prevention program is on healthy people. For schools, where young people are learning and developing into adults, the purpose of prevention is therefore to help students acquire the skills and environmental support to remain healthy, responsible, and free of problems that will cause later harm.

Education and mental health programs have emphasized prevention for more than half a century, yet few resources have been committed to prevention programs for aggression and violence. The focus has been on children at risk for academic failure, and with reading and health problems, rather than on the prevention of behavioral problems. A number of reasons exist for the lack of support for prevention programs:

- A belief that bullying and aggression are normal developmental processes

- A conviction that "those students" will "grow out of it"

- An understanding that most children do develop into healthy adults and that money spent on unproven prevention plans may not be cost-effective

- A respect for the family and the belief that teaching appropriate behavior is a family matter

- An assumption that the problem "isn't that big" and is not worth the effort necessary to introduce prevention programs

The escalating violence in schools and the extreme levels to which bullying has developed in some schools in recent years are causing many to rethink the situation. In addition to the question of safety and the right to be able to attend school without fear, rising economic costs are associated with bullying and other forms of aggression. The costs of incarcerating a young person in a juvenile detention center are considerably higher than those of providing a positive educational environment. The costs involved in settling lawsuits are also staggering, and more and more parents are resorting to legal means to ensure that their children's schools are safe. Finally, for some schools that have failed to implement effective guidelines covering harassment and other violations of students' civil rights, the loss of federal funding is threatened. From a cost-benefit standpoint alone, then, preventing problems is superior to treating them.

SCHOOL CHARACTERISTICS

School attendance is required in the United States. When children are required to be in a particular environment, they have a right to safety in that environment, as well as to the skills necessary to maneuver through life as they get older. Ideally, school policy should include input from all constituents—administrators, teachers and other school personnel, parents, students. Some school characteristics and aspects of school policy are particularly influential in bullying.

Administrator Qualities

Certain characteristics of the school administration are associated with greater or lesser degrees of aggression (Goldstein, 1999). Specifically, low-aggression schools have administrators who exhibit the following qualities:

- They are highly visible and available to students and teachers.

- They have an effective "intelligence network" (i.e., they know what is happening in the school).

- They have procedures for fair and consistent response to grievances (both student and staff).

- They support and empower teachers.

- They recognize problems in the school and rapidly take steps to address them.

In contrast, violence and aggression are more frequent in schools where the administration is either too strict (autocratic) or too lax (laissiez faire); impersonal, arbitrary, or inconsistent; characterized by overuse of punishment as a means of control; and weak or inconsistent in support for faculty. To prevent bullying, school administrators should strive toward the first list of qualities.

Zero Tolerance

The cardinal rule in prevention of bullying is a simple one: Establish a *zero tolerance policy,* meaning that no bullying in any form will be tolerated. This policy position may be confusing or appear overly strict to some educators. Such individuals reason that because it is impossible to eliminate all bullying, a zero-tolerance policy makes no sense. On the other hand, we know that aggression has a tendency to escalate and that students will test the limits to see how far they can go before being challenged or experiencing a consequence. The higher the beginning level of aggression accepted, the higher students will be able to push. Those who advocate zero tolerance prefer to start with the assumption that no level of bullying is acceptable. If a comparable situation occurred in the adult realm, the logic of this type of reasoning would be apparent: What level of aggression would we tolerate each day in the work setting? The answer is plainly none.

A Schoolwide Commitment to Reducing Aggression

It is important for school faculty to establish a schoolwide orientation toward reducing bullying and other forms of aggression. If one or two teachers attempt to bring about change in their classrooms, but the school norm is to allow bullying to continue, the teachers will find change very difficult. If there is unity throughout the school and the systemwide message is that bullying is unacceptable anywhere, reductions are more likely. In one school in which we worked, the faculty found it useful to post "no bullying" signs throughout the building.

TEACHER CHARACTERISTICS

In addition to aspects of the broader school environment, certain teacher characteristics affect the bullying situation, for better or worse.

Modeling

Children are in school for a large portion of their waking lives and are in constant contact with teachers. These teachers are models for their students (Bandura, 1986; Besag, 1989). A "hidden curriculum" is at work in the schools, and students are highly sensitive to cues on how to conduct themselves. How teachers behave toward one another and toward students, as well as the behaviors they reinforce, are monitored and witnessed by students. Students look to their teachers for guidance and for a code of conduct for treatment of others. As we have said, teachers have an innate power to set precedents and guide behaviors in the classroom: If teachers show respect for others, students are more likely to do the same.

Teacher Self-Efficacy

Teacher self-efficacy is the belief that one can successfully bring about desired outcomes in one's students (Bandura, 1986; Gibson & Dembo, 1984). In interviews with teachers, we found that those teachers with high self-efficacy had fewer incidents of bullying in their classrooms. If teachers have appropriate skills and adequate incentives, their sense of self-efficacy is a major determinant in how they choose classroom activities, how much effort they will put forth, and how long they will sustain effort when dealing with difficult students. In fact, teacher self-efficacy may be the single most powerful explanatory variable in student performance. Teachers must not only believe that the interventions they are suggesting can be effective, they must also have confidence in their ability to implement these interventions effectively. Teachers with a high sense of self-efficacy take personal responsibility for their students and their learning; when their students fail or have difficulty, they examine their own performance and look for ways they might make their teaching more effective.

Positive Expectations

You probably know the saying "In teaching, you get what you expect." Teachers with expectations that students can and will perform well find that, in fact, their students generally do. Some refer to this phenomenon as a "self-fulfilling prophecy." We have seen different teachers work with the same student and get very different results, depending upon whether the teacher approached the student with positive or negative expectations. In both cases, the teachers obtained from the student the behaviors they expected.

It is important to have positive expectations about your own ability to teach and influence the growth of students; it is also important that you have positive expectations and beliefs about your students. Students are able to read their teachers' attitudes toward them and know whether confidence and hope or negativity and low expectations exist. Finding the strengths and positive attributes of all students is vital to effective teaching.

Be aware that your attitude will determine whether your intervention is helpful and/or therapeutic or merely a power struggle. Teachers almost always lose power struggles with students. Even if a teacher wins the battle with a student, he or she will often find that the student wants to "get even" or exact revenge. Also, if the power struggle is public, other students see that the only way the teacher can control a situation is through the use of power, not through prevention, mediation, or problem solving.

The good news is that by developing more experience and skills in particular areas such as bullying, teachers become more confident in their ability to influence students and effect change. An increased sense of self-efficacy then leads to more positive expectations for the students with whom teachers work, improved classroom climate, and better rapport with students.

Presentation Style

How teachers present themselves to students can make a difference in how those students respond to both teachers and to one another. Teachers can elicit students' interest and increase their authority if they convey confidence through their posture, gestures, and tone of voice. Teachers with low levels of classroom bullying vary their presentation style so as to avoid monotony. They also walk around the room and make eye contact with students; doing so increases the group's feeling of cohesion and also allows teachers to monitor classroom behavior.

Physical presence is particularly important with bullies and victims. Initially, highly aggressive students will indicate a dislike for having a teacher close by and touching them, but when the teacher demonstrates caring and support—a fair relationship rather than a punitive one—they generally respond much more positively to the teacher's presence.

RECOMMENDATIONS FOR PREVENTING BULLYING AND VICTIMIZATION

In addition to becoming aware of school factors and teacher characteristics that play a role in bullying and victimization, as a teacher you can have a direct impact by putting certain practices into effect. The following are a number of "hands-on" ways you can improve your classroom's climate.

Establish and Enforce Classroom Rules

We have touched on the the importance of establishing and enforcing classroom rules in earlier modules, but it is worth underscoring the importance of rules again here, as relates to prevention. Here are some "rules for rules":

- Define and communicate classroom rules for students in specific and behavioral terms (e.g., "Raise your hand before asking a question").

- Tell students what to do (e.g., take turns, talk over disagreements) rather than what not to do (e.g., don't fight, stop yelling).

- Keep rules short and few in number, and post them where they can be seen clearly.

- Encourage students to take an active role in rule development, modification, and implementation. Rule adherence is better when students have participated in this process.

- Have students sign a written contract stating that they will comply with the rules.

- Be able to give a rationale for why each rule is needed. A good rationale for having rules in general is that because everyone is required to be in school, we are responsible for making sure school is a safe place for everyone.

- Develop and implement rules early on, from the start of the school year.

- Make sure the rules are fair and that they apply equally.

- Be certain the rules are understood. When students don't understand, rules are difficult to enforce.

- Spell out reasonable consequences in advance. Just as adults don't like "surprise consequences" for their behavior, students want to know what consequences will be.

- Apply the rules and consequences consistently. We don't want traffic tickets that vary based upon the police officer's mood: We want predictability, as do students.

In identifying consequences, it is important to identify undesirable behaviors (e.g., teasing, name-calling, pushing, taunting). This should be part of a class discussion: Why are these behaviors undesirable? What can we do instead of these behaviors, particularly to lead us to work together more cooperatively and show respect? What should happen if these behaviors do occur? After the class has had this discussion, establish consequences that "fit the present offense." Implement consequences directly following the offense; do not keep a running tally of offenses, then implement a consequence. Finally, direct the negative consequence at the undesirable act, not the person. A teacher might say, for example, "Janet, because you teased Patricia and called her names, you are required to stay after school for detention."

Rules can be succinct, but they do need to be understood by all, and consequences for failure to comply with the rules should be consistently applied. One problem many students have is coming from homes with inconsistent applications of rules and consequences. These students especially need consistency at school. In addition, we must model the behavior we want from our students. This includes "saying what we mean and meaning what we say." If we cannot or will not enforce a rule, then we probably should not have the rule in the first place. Our lack of consistency teaches students that we are not as sincere or as committed to student well-being as our rules might imply.

We should point out here that students can understand some inconsistency in the administration of rules. They also recognize—often better than adults—the diversity in their peers and know that everyone has different strengths and weaknesses. However, when teachers are arbitrary in their applications of rules, students quite rightly perceive this as unfair. The issue of fairness is extremely important to young people, and fairness should be a primary concern. If there is a reason for rules to be applied inconsistently, it needs to be explained to students. In our work with one class, the teacher explained why the consequences for a child who had AD/HD (attention deficit/hyperactivity disorder) were different from those for two other children who were class bullies. The children who were bullies demonstrated some of the same disturbing characteristics as the child with AD/HD (e.g., overactivity, getting out of seat), but they had very different reasons for the behaviors. The classmates understood and accepted the differences.

Manage Transitions

It is helpful to use a consistent signal to indicate that the day's lesson is commencing or a transition is about to occur. This provides a cue for the students about the expected behavior. Some teachers have used signals such as turning the lights off, clapping hands, or, for younger students, singing to indicate a transition to another activity. Such signals help students to prepare for and predict what will happen next, as well as to perform activities in the time allowed. The procedure works best when the practice has been instituted early in the school year and when teachers have explained why the routine has been developed and what the expectations are. Having the class participate in developing these and other routines as the year proceeds will facilitate student cooperation when the techniques are implemented.

Understand Your Response to Conflicts

Each teacher is unique, and each has a unique way of managing bullying behavior in the classroom. Kreidler (1984) has developed a method to assess the manner in which teachers approach conflicts in their classrooms. Specifically, he has identified the following different methods:

1. *No-nonsense approach:* I do not give in to students. Students need firm guidance in learning acceptable versus unacceptable behavior (e.g., make a disciplinary referral, tell students to sit down and begin their assignment).

2. *Problem-solving approach:* I set up a situation in which the students and I can solve the problem together (e.g., try to find out what the real problem is, encourage students to find alternative solutions).

3. *Negotiating approach:* I teach the students to listen to one another and then assist them in reaching a compromise (e.g., mediate, help students understand one another's point of view).

4. *Smoothing approach:* I prefer my classroom to be calm and peaceful whenever possible. Often student conflicts are insignificant, so I try to redirect students (e.g., divert attention from the conflict, get everyone involved in doing something else).

5. *Ignoring approach:* I indicate limits and allow students to work out conflicts on their own. It is important that they learn the consequences of their behavior (e.g., let students fight it out as long as no one gets hurt, tell them to settle it on their own time).

We do not support or encourage the ignoring approach. Too often, it allows bullying to continue and gives students the impression that the teacher sanctions the behavior or does not care about their safety.

Teachers have told us that identifying their approach toward dealing with specific bullying incidents has helped them adjust their style and prevent further problems. If you share these approaches with a colleague or among your Support Team, you will see just how different teachers' responses to conflict can be. We encourage you to discuss the following questions:

- In what situations would each of these approaches be most useful?

- Are there certain approaches you would recommend using over others?

- Which approach do you use most often?

Get to Know Your Students

Take time at the beginning of the school year, and continue throughout the year, to get to know your students as individuals. We all like personal attention—to be recognized as individuals. Children respond to this as well. Take time to develop a relationship with each child beyond the relationship you have with the class as a whole. Developing a special relationship with each child will increase the level of trust between you and the child, which in turn may help the child seek you out in times of need. Also, the child may feel an increased sense of responsibility or wish to please you, thus decreasing the likelihood of acting out in the class.

Encourage Student Participation

The more engaged and involved students are in their lessons, the less opportunity they have to participate in undesirable activities/behaviors. Allow students to interact and participate in lessons. Classroom activities that promote collaboration provide the opportunity for students to learn from one another and to learn the importance of working with other people. More active learning provides greater involvement and commitment to the experience.

Build Self-Esteem and Confidence

Helping students feel good about themselves can go a long way in preventing bullying in the classroom. Students need the opportunity to explore activities they enjoy and are successful doing. You can help students find activities that support their individual growth and development: math, soccer, public speaking, computers, and so forth. Or, when teaching a new activity, you can encourage students to set small, achievable goals. This lets them experience success along the way.

Small groups can also promote self-development and a sense of personal worth. In them, students can practice social skills and learn about who they are and what is important to them—their likes and dislikes, values, and goals.

Facilitate Communication

We all know that improving communication can lead to better relationships and fewer problematic interactions. One teacher with whom we worked had always focused on teaching subject matter and took little time to address the social aspects of learning. When she began to spend a few minutes at the beginning of each class welcoming students and then discussing issues they brought up, she found the students responded more positively and actually got more work done. Being empathic with students is not inconsistent with their getting work done; in fact, it can actually be of benefit. If a student complains, for example, "This math is too hard and boring," a teacher might reply, "I agree, it is tough to learn. I struggled, too. But it is important, and we're in this together, so let's move on. Next problem."

Students can become active problem solvers if they learn how to communicate. Some courses lend themselves particularly well to the teaching of communication skills. Literature, for example, is a natural because its main subject is human interaction. History also illustrates the effects of poor communication, the result in some cases being political uprising or war. If it is impractical to integrate communication skills training in certain curriculum areas, the school counselor might conduct a program on the topic. Impromptu activities often lend themselves to spontaneous communication skills training, though. For example, if two students appear to be in conflict, this may be a perfect opportunity to have them practice effective listening skills.

One model we use is the "Intending-Impacting" model, which students understand very well. If we have two students and one is speaking to the other, the first student intends to send a message to the second student and expects that message to have a certain impact. The second student may or may not be impacted the way the first student intended.

Student A-Intent   **Student B-Impact**

Here's how this might sound in practice:

Student A: That's a pretty outfit. (Intent: To compliment the second student on her clothing.)

Student B: Thank you, I just got it. (Impact: The second student heard the message as intended.)

However, if Student A is trying to be complimentary but in fact does not like the second student, Student A's tone of voice may come across as sarcastic. The message Student B receives will be distorted. He or she may still take the message as a compliment and be pleased, may take the message as a sarcastic comment and become angry, or may not be able to read the mixed message (compliment with sarcasm) and be confused.

Student A-Intent   **Student B-Impact**

Distortion also may occur on the part of the receiver, Student B. If Student A sends Student B a message, but Student B distorts the message, it will not have the impact intended by Student A. If, for example, Student B does not like her own new outfit, she may not appreciate the compliment, or if Student B has been criticized by Student A in the past, the current compliment may be perceived as a put down. Another possibility is that Student B may have just had a very bad morning and, although Student A intended to be positive, Student B may still hear the message in a distorted way, resulting in Student A's intention not having the desired impact.

Student A-Intent   **Student B-Impact**

This communication skills approach can be taught in several classes. Students can use role-plays to practice being sender, receiver, and observer. Some good situations to role-play are as follows:

- How to share an opinion without upsetting others

- How to communicate in situations involving conflict

- How nonverbal communication can cause problems

- How to listen to others

If teachers can consistently help students identify the intent and impact of the messages they send and receive, the result will be better communication for all. This approach is particularly effective with bullies because it helps them understand how their messages may be misperceived even when their intent is positive. Bullies often perceive the world as being against them, and this exercise can work toward their establishing a more accurate world view.

Use Cooperative Learning Techniques

A great way to prevent bullying is to integrate cooperative learning activities into your classroom curriculum. Such activities require students to cooperate in order to solve problems or achieve goals. It is best if the task group is heterogeneous (i.e., a mix of bullies and victims). If bullies can learn to work with less powerful students, both will benefit. Several of the classroom activities at the end of this module involve teamwork and cooperation.

Years of work examining the generalization of learning indicate clearly that what has been learned does not generalize well unless specific steps are taken to address the transfer of learning. It is important for students to see how cooperating on academic tasks relates to other situations, such as playing together, engaging in sports, expressing school spirit, and so on. Whenever possible, discuss with students ways their cooperative learning experiences might generalize from the academic to the social realm. Stress that the success of each group member depends on the success of all, and point out the fun of addressing situations cooperatively rather than competitively.

Establish a Buddy System

One way to reduce "others versus us" thinking, which can lead to bullying and victimization, is through the establishment of a buddy system. Teachers have shared with us that they have had tremendous success using a buddy system for new students. When paired with an experienced peer, students just entering school are able to make a much easier transition, while the student buddies take on a leadership role. The senior member can introduce the new student to peers and teachers, show the student around the school, and help in choosing after-school activities, clubs, and so forth. Buddies can also meet in small groups to discuss problems and seek advice and support.

Facilitate Parent Involvement

Parent involvement is a critical factor in preventing bullying. The more parents learn, the more they are able to become involved. When that involvement can be channeled into support for common goals, everyone benefits. Some general suggestions follow:

- Establish a relationship with each student's guardian/parent early in the year, before any problems arise.

- Keep parents informed of the student's progress, both positive and negative, via phone, letter, or conference. Be sure to let parents know when the child has performed well in addition to notifying them of behavioral difficulties.

- Encourage parents to understand the importance of consistently modeling at home the behaviors they want from the child at school.

- Encourage parents to support their child (e.g., check homework on a regular basis, provide time each day to let the child talk about his or her day).

- Encourage parents to use consistent reinforcement and disciplinary techniques.

- Provide workshops, seminars, or other opportunities for parents to seek new information and skills.

Most parents care a great deal about the behavior of their children, both at school and at home. However, some parents are unaware of the behavioral expectations schools have established for students and do not recognize that their children have problems at school. We have worked extensively with parents who expect their children to use aggression to settle conflicts or who take pride in the extent of aggression their children show. We also have seen parents so inattentive to the behavior of their children that they simply do not see their children's problems.

The different expectations for behavior between the school and the family can be difficult to resolve and even seem like a "culture clash" when expectations are very dissimilar. It is important to remember that children are bright enough to figure out how to behave in different settings. Students know they behave differently at church or temple than they do on the playground at school. They know they behave differently around some people than they do around others. They also have the capacity to learn to behave differently at home and at school. So, even though family members may tolerate or even support aggressive behavior at home, there is no need to lower our standards and expectations at school.

School standards should be explained to parents in clear terms with examples provided. If conflicts develop about the school program, these should be discussed openly and frankly. Teachers may need to explain their respect for family values and also discuss the flexibility students have in learning ways to behave at home and at school. However, teachers should remain firm. One conversation between teacher and parent went went like this:

Teacher: So, at school we have a no-hitting policy, no bullying. Nothing that causes pain and injury to classmates. Our class behavior is based on showing respect for all people and treating classmates with dignity.

Father: I understand how they aren't to hit each other, but if anyone hits my son, he's expected to hit back and settle the matter. No one pushes our family around and gets away with it.

Teacher: I understand. That's one of the reasons we have the no-hitting policy—we don't fight in our school. If someone initiates a fight with your son, we will take steps to stop it immediately, but he needs to understand the no-fighting rule in our school.

USING YOUR SUPPORT TEAM

Participating on the Support Team reduced my fear of having to deal with the bullying problems in my classroom alone. I had the chance to talk to other teachers who gave me advice that was priceless.

—Sixth-grade teacher

Everyone involved with education agrees that schools should be safe places, free from bullying and victimization. The Support Team is an organized body with the expertise to help make that wish become reality. Your Support Team is one of the most effective tools you have to prevent bullying and victimization. Not only do team members provide collegial support for one another, they discuss dilemmas, share experiences, and learn from their successes or failures. The support group contributes to keeping teachers actively involved in the prevention of school bullying. Our experience has been that teachers who work together on a Support Team creatively develop new and exciting ways of carrying out prevention efforts. The team can also have an impact beyond its membership, influencing other teachers in the school as well as school administration at the building level and higher.

CONTENT REVIEW

The following statements refer to the learning goals of this module. Take a minute to think about the statements. Ask yourself whether you feel confident that you can say yes to each. If not, take some time to revisit those topics and consider ways to strengthen your learning.

I am aware that peer mediation is an effective strategy to help students resolve conflicts in a peaceful way.	Yes ❏	No ❏
I understand the rationale behind preventing bullying and victimization before they occur.	Yes ❏	No ❏
I am aware that characteristics of the school, the teacher, and the classroom influence bullying, for better or worse.	Yes ❏	No ❏
I know why having consequences for all levels of bullying (zero tolerance) is important in preventing future occurrences.	Yes ❏	No ❏

I believe I have the knowledge and ability to influence my students through my teaching and classroom behavior.   Yes ❑   No ❑

I have confidence that my students are able to learn respectful, cooperative behavior and expect them to do so.   Yes ❑   No ❑

I have developed and clearly posted classroom rules to create a respectful and consistent environment.   Yes ❑   No ❑

I have attempted to develop individual relationships with the children in my classroom in order to become familiar with their unique needs.   Yes ❑   No ❑

I am aware that cooperative learning strategies can help my students generalize the concept of teamwork to their daily lives.   Yes ❑   No ❑

I am familiar with techniques to improve communication among students in my classroom.   Yes ❑   No ❑

I have developed ways to interact with my students' parents to maximize the effects of my prevention efforts.   Yes ❑   No ❑

I am an active member of my school's bully prevention Support Team.   Yes ❑   No ❑

A Reminder . . .

CLASSROOM INTERACTION AND AWARENESS CHART

Use the CIAC to describe any bullying behavior you observe (and that students report to you, if you wish). Specific instructions for filling out the CIAC appear in Appendix D, along with a blank copy of the chart.

THE BIG QUESTIONS

Focus yourself and honestly appraise your progress by asking yourself the "Big Questions." There are no right or wrong answers.

As regards prevention of bullying and victimization:

1. What is my goal?

2. What am I doing?

3. Is what I am doing helping me achieve my goal?

4. *(If not)* What can I do differently?

PERSONAL GOALS FORM

The Personal Goals Form, on the next page, is designed to help you tailor the content of this module to your own students and situation. If you have not filled out the form as you worked through the information component of the module, please take a moment to do so now.

Personal Goals Form

GOALS

- To understand the need for and basic principles of prevention

- To become aware of school characteristics that affect bullying

- To become aware of teacher characteristics that influence bullying

- To learn specific "hands-on" ways to prevent bullying and victimization in the classroom

1. My role in preventing bullying and victimization:

   _____

   _____

2. I have observed bullying incidents in my classroom that might have been prevented. *(Please record incidents on the Classroom Interaction and Awareness Chart. Under "Interventions," specify both your immediate response and an idea for preventing such incidents in the future.)*

3. I will conduct the following classroom activities to help my students continue to develop their awareness of bullying/victimization and their commitment to change.

   _____

   _____

4. I will evaluate the effectiveness of these activities by (a) recording incidents on the CIAC to see if there is a reduction across time, (b) monitoring the extent to which students report bullying situations, and (c) recording my impressions of change in the classroom environment. *(Please indicate any other means of evaluation in the space below.)*

   _____

   _____

5. I will give students feedback on their progress by (a) sharing the number and types of incidents recorded on the CIAC and (b) encouraging classroom discussion of these incidents and related issues. *(Please indicate any other means of feedback in the space below.)*

   _____

   _____

6. I will share my experiences in applying the information in this module with members of my Support Team, other teachers, administrators, parents. *(Please specify who and when in the space below. Include ideas for sharing information with parents and obtaining their support.)*

   _____

   _____

Classroom Activities

NO "I" IN TEAM

Students are more likely to adhere to rules if they agree upon and understand the necessity for them. This activity allows students to be active participants in developing classroom rules; they then work as teams to maintain positive behavior inside and outside of the classroom.

BUILDING AN EMPIRE

This group activity allows students to experiment with working cooperatively and to recognize different work styles and nonverbal means of communication.

CROSSING THE BRIDGE

Working as a team and communicating clearly are beneficial both inside and outside of school. This activity requires students to achieve a physical goal. Teams must work together to achieve this goal.

HOW MUCH IS IT WORTH?

In this activity, groups of students bid, as in an auction, on values that they feel are important. Participating in and discussing this activity help underscore the importance of establishing and adhering to values.

No "I" in TEAM

OBJECTIVES

- To help students take responsibility for developing and following classroom rules
- To encourage students to work together to follow classroom rules

MATERIALS

- Posterboard and marker
- Chalkboard or easel pad

DIRECTIONS

1. Work with students to create a list of rules for the classroom. Together, assign a point value to each behavior (e.g., respectful behavior toward a classmate = 5 points). Keep the list of rules and point values posted in the classroom so everyone can see it.

2. Divide the class into two teams. Write the names of the members of each team on the chalkboard or easel pad. Explain that each team begins the week with 50 points. If a member of the team breaks a rule, the specified number of points will be deducted. The team with the highest number of points at the end of the week wins a prize (e.g., extra free time, popcorn party or other treat).

3. Process the activity by asking the following questions.

DISCUSSION

- Why is important to work in teams in our world today?

- We like to select our teammates, but that is not always possible. What can you do to ensure cooperation among team members, even if you prefer different teammates?

- When someone on your team does not carry his or her share of the work, how can you encourage that person to contribute to the team?

- What are some things you did in your team to encourage participation and cooperation? Which parts worked? Which didn't? Why?

Building an Empire

OBJECTIVES

- To help students work together
- To allow students to become aware of one another's nonverbal communication
- To recognize and appreciate differences in people's work patterns

MATERIALS

- Several bags of gumdrops
- A box of toothpicks

DIRECTIONS

1. Divide the classroom into groups of three. Provide each group with 25 gumdrops and a handful of toothpicks.

2. Instruct each group to build a structure with the gumdrops and toothpicks. (Group members are not permitted to talk during this exercise.)

3. After groups have completed their structures, conduct a class discussion, using the following questions.

DISCUSSION

- What was it like having to work as a group?
- Was it challenging to work together and not talk? (Have the groups share experiences.)
- How did you communicate if you were not allowed to talk?
- Could you still understand one another without talking? How?
- Did you notice differences in how your teammates worked? If so, what were they?
- Are there certain situations in which you express your thoughts or feelings toward someone without saying a word? Name one.

Crossing the Bridge

OBJECTIVES

- To work cooperatively as a team to achieve a goal
- To build communication skills

MATERIALS

- Approximately 30 sheets of construction paper

DIRECTIONS

1. Divide the class into groups of six. Take seven pieces of construction paper (one for each group member, plus one additional piece) and place each on the ground in a semicircle.

2. Ask each group member to stand on a piece of paper, leaving the middle piece of paper empty. The students should stand facing the middle piece of paper.

3. The objective is to have each student make it "across the bridge" to the opposite side: When members have crossed the bridge, the middle piece of paper should once again be empty. The team must work together to find the best way to do this.

4. When students have finished, process the activity by asking the following questions.

DISCUSSION

- How did it feel to work together as a team?
- What would happen if one person did not cooperate?
- Did you find this activity easy or difficult? In what way?
- What would you have done differently?

How Much Is It Worth?

OBJECTIVES

- To allow students to determine what values are most important to them in their relationships

- To enable teacher and students to develop classroom values and to incorporate them into daily interactions

MATERIALS

- Chalkboard or easel pad

- Play money

- Values list (compiled by teacher and students)

DIRECTIONS

1. Announce to the class that you will be conducting an auction. Divide the classroom into four groups (each group a mix of boys and girls).

2. Provide each group with 500 dollars of play money to be used at the auction.

3. Take the role of the auctioneer: On the chalkboard or easel pad, write a list of the values to be auctioned. Examples include friendship, honesty, respect, appreciation of diversity, creativity, spontaneity, athletic ability. Incorporate any other values you feel are pertinent to your students and situation. Ask the students if they would like to add any to the list before starting the auction.

4. Go through the list of values, one value at a time. After you read the value aloud, the groups can begin bidding. The group with the highest bid can purchase the value. Complete this process with each value.

5. After all of the values have been auctioned and purchased, conduct a class discussion.

DISCUSSION

- What values are most important to you and why?

- Have these values always been important to you?

- Which values would you be willing to trade for another value?

- Do all people have these values?

- Are there any values that were not auctioned that you would have liked to purchase? For what price?

MODULE

7 Relaxation and Coping Skills

OVERVIEW

Stress, both positive and negative, is an inevitable part of life and an unavoidable component of teaching. How we deal with stress has a profound effect on our ability to teach our students and on our own development, both personal and professional. This module has been designed to help you understand and cope with your stress, but you will also learn activities to help your students learn relaxation and coping skills. The more efficiently you manage your own stress, the more effective you will be in your professional and personal life.

GOALS

- To become aware of stress and its effects

- To acquire knowledge about general ways to manage stress

- To learn steps to manage on-the-job stress

- To learn specific relaxation techniques to reduce stress on a daily basis

STRESS AWARENESS

We experience numerous stressors in our lives each day, both positive and negative in nature. Stress is cumulative, continually building up until we either erupt or do something about it. Usually, it is not until we are overwhelmed, fatigued, or distraught that we decide to take action. The best way to deal with stress is to become aware of it, then devise a plan for change. Teachers have shared with us that taking the time to identify personal and professional stressors and to make reasonable changes leads to greater satisfaction in both their personal and professional lives.

We experience stress on any one of three different levels: physical, cognitive, and emotional. Responses on these three levels work together in creating and maintaining stress.

Physical

Take a moment to think how your body feels when you become stressed. Does your heart start to beat faster? Does your breathing became shallower? Do you feel shaky or nauseous? Each of these is a symptom your body may produce under stress. Behaviors that might accompany these physical symptoms might include complaining to colleagues, having a headache, overeating, or working inefficiently.

Cognitive

Consider for a moment the thoughts that run through your mind when you are feeling stressed. Your mind may begin to race with negative messages that perpetuate or increase your level of stress. Common thoughts teachers express are "What a waste of time," "I wish I didn't have to do this," and "I feel unsafe."

Emotional

Usually, we experience a number of feelings when we are stressed. Which words are most descriptive of your own feelings: *anxious, angry, frustrated, tired, bored?* Identifying your feelings will help you decide how best to confront your stress. Do you feel irritable and snappy? If so, you might look into an exercise program to help you drain off some energy in a positive way. If you are feeling exhausted, you could think of ways to rejuvenate yourself. If you are feeling bored, you could try doing something new to break the monotony.

After completing this [module], I learned a few things about myself that I was unaware of. First, I learned that much of the stress and aggravation [in] my classroom, such as students talking out of turn, not having sufficient time to complete the day's lesson, and verbally harassing one another, stemmed from my neglect to consistently follow and remind students of the classroom rules. Second, I learned that having some stress in my life is OK. . . . It helps me stay motivated. . . . It keeps me on track.

—Seventh-grade teacher

GENERAL RECOMMENDATIONS FOR MANAGING STRESS

Sometimes a very simple change in the way you live your life can have a profound effect on your level of stress, as well as that of your students. Some of the recommendations that follow may seem obvious, but often we forget how important they are.

Take Time to Relax

Teachers
Teachers often tell us they have too much to do to be able to take time for themselves. All day, you devote yourself to your students. It is easy for your energy and enthusiasm to be depleted if you do not take time to replenish yourself. It is unlikely that time will appear miraculously in your daily schedule; you will need to plan consciously to give yourself time. What do you enjoy doing that you have not done in a long time? Sit quietly and read a book? Go to the coffee shop and a read a magazine? See a movie? Take a long walk in the park? Today is the start of a new day. Take some time to relax.

Students
Although many adults say things like "What do kids have to worry about?" and "It must be nice to be young and carefree with no worries

in the world," youth today are experiencing increased stress and pressure from their families, communities, and the culture at large. It can be challenging for youth to cope with stress, especially when they may lack the skills to do so. You can serve as a role model by demonstrating positive ways to cope with stress. You can also give your students the right to relax and do something they love. Have each write down several activities that he or she enjoys and finds calming and relaxing. Ask your students to try to do one of these activities at least four times a week. Perhaps you can set up a "Chillin' Chart" in your classroom, on which you include each child's name and stars for engaging in relaxation activities. Involve parents and encourage them to understand and support their child's need for this time.

Take a Daily Dose of Humor

Teachers

When we are stressed, we lose our sense of humor and our ability to laugh. Next time a situation does not have the outcome you desire, instead of becoming angry and frustrated, try to find the humor in the situation—in other words, laugh it off. Laughter is an excellent way to release stress and change your level of tension and the tension in your environment.

Students

Kids need to exercise their humor as well. They need to laugh and let learning be fun. Teach your students to use their humor and laugh. If they are able to laugh together in a classroom, maybe they will be less likely to release their stress through aggression. Invite your students to share their sense of humor. Encourage them to tell appropriate funny stories, and share yours as well. Model laughing for your class. If it is OK for you to crack a smile and enjoy what you are doing, they will follow in your footsteps.

Exercise

Teachers

Exercise has been shown to reduce the chance of heart attacks, strokes, and arteriosclerosis. Incorporating moderate exercise into your daily routine is also an effective way to reduce stress. It serves as an emotional outlet for the release of anger and frustration, and also prevents stressors from becoming overwhelming. Exercise can be an ideal way to "blow off some steam," or it can be a private time to make sense of what is bothering you.

Students

Students also benefit by incorporating exercise into their daily routine. Youth today watch many hours of television, the majority of which include models of aggression and violence. At the same time, our students have become less physically active. By encouraging students to leave television and computer games behind and become physically active instead, we can help them release negative energy. This release can prevent them from using this energy against other children as well as help to reduce their level of stress.

Don't Take Your Work Home

Teachers

Teachers share with us that in fantasyland this sounds great, but in reality there are just not enough hours in the day to accomplish everything. We can relate to this. Remember, though, not only may you deserve a break, you may *need* a break. If you do need to work at home, set limits for yourself. For example, you may decide you are most effective from 6 to 8 P.M. Use this specific time to concentrate on your work. Setting reasonable limits may reduce feelings of stress or guilt about taking time for yourself instead of doing school-related work.

Students

Your students will also benefit if you help them schedule their homework. Homework is inevitable; however, students may perform better if they have a consistent time in which to do it. Some parents prefer their children to finish their homework immediately after school; others, after their chores are complete. In class, you can have your students decide what time will work best and encourage them to draw up a contract with a place for three signatures: child, teacher, parent. Have each student take the contract home and discuss it with his or her parents. All should sign the contract in agreement. Having a set homework period can reduce the tension and arguments that may arise between parents and children.

Keep a Gratitude Book

Teachers

Sometimes it is easy to lose sight of the things we are grateful for in our lives. We become engrossed with our daily chores, tasks, commitments, rituals, and so forth, and we often fail to stop and think about the wonderful people and things that surround us. Keeping a gratitude book will help increase your optimism and put your daily stressors in perspective. Keeping such a book is quite simple. Just write down three things a day for which you are grateful and take time to relive/reexperience these positive moments.

Students

Likewise, it is helpful for students to recognize the things for which they are thankful. Each week, you can have your students write down the three things for which they are grateful. Create a special bulletin board to display the many people, situations, gifts, and characteristics students appreciate. If a student has problems with this activity (and some may), talk to the student individually and ask what is happening that makes it difficult for him or her to think of positive events. It is possible the student is experiencing depression or other serious problems and may need to be referred to the school counselor or social worker.

Use Your Support Team

Teachers

The Support Team serves as an ongoing resource to dispel fears, help teachers feel supported, and encourage collaborative problem solving. Sharing and communication are central to the team's purpose and can be very effective in reducing stress. Use your Support Team. Working together to bring about change in the school is much more effective than working alone: The team can accomplish goals that individuals may be unable to reach.

Students

Encourage your students to use peer mediation and to create their own student support teams to deal with bullying and other stressful situations. Remind them that your door is always open to discuss their stress as well as their experiences with bullying.

STEPS FOR DEALING WITH ON-THE-JOB STRESS

When the costs outweigh the rewards, when the frowns outnumber the smiles, and when the boredom outbalances the excitement, you are likely experiencing a kind of stress called *burnout*. Certain signs are associated with burnout: negative attitude, frustration, anger, exhaustion, and physiological changes such as headaches, sleeplessness, or overeating or undereating.

Burnout usually does not occur from excessive amounts of teaching; rather, it occurs because teachers are no longer feeling rewarded by their efforts. When your needs are no longer being met, when you are no longer achieving your goals, and when you no longer find enjoyment in activities that once were enjoyable, step back from your work and ask yourself, "What inspired me to enter this profession?" and "When I felt I was at my prime, what was I doing then that I may be neglecting now?" Taking the following steps will help you manage your on-the-job stress.

Identify Your Symptoms

- I feel negative about my job.

- I feel frustrated in carrying out daily responsibilities.

- I am impatient with my colleagues or students.

- I feel indifferent about the needs of my students.

- I feel physically and emotionally exhausted.

The first step in managing your stress is to identify the symptoms related to stress. How many of the preceding statements can you answer in the affirmative? Are you experiencing other symptoms? Remember, we respond to stress at three levels: Our symptoms may be physical, cognitive, and/or emotional.

Identify the Source of the Stress

- I have difficulty solving problems as they arise.

- I feel trapped in a situation without any real say.

- I feel underqualified for tasks I am expected to perform.

- I have too much to do and not enough time to accomplish it.

- The environment in which I work seems hazardous at times.

- I complete work-related activities on my personal time.

Typically, we react to situations immediately, without exploring the underlying causes. For example, you might feel you are reacting to a particular student's misbehavior, but you really may be reacting to all of the incidents that have been piling up throughout the day.

When you are feeling frustrated, it is difficult to remain objective. To gain perspective, take several deep breaths and try to identify what is occurring before reacting in a stressful situation. Try to step out of your own shoes and see your situation as someone else would. Then ask yourself, "What exactly is bothering me?" Look for underlying reasons, themes, and patterns to determine exactly what it may be that causes you frustration. The statements listed at the beginning of this section reflect such underlying issues. One or more of them may apply to you.

Formulate a Plan

In the introduction to this book, we emphasized how important it is for teachers to set themselves and their students up for success. The same principle applies in managing stress: Develop a plan ahead of time to help yourself cope. If you overwhelm yourself with unrealistic goals, the outcome will be negative, so try to keep your goals within reach. Specifically, any goal you set should be observable, achievable within a certain time span, and structured in incremental steps. Ideally, short-term goals should lead to a larger long-term goal, and you should reward yourself in some way for reaching each goal you set.

If you find yourself focusing on critical thoughts about faculty meetings, for example, you might set yourself the goal of thinking more constructively. Instead of telling yourself, "This faculty meeting is such a waste of time. I could be getting my own work done," you could say, "Faculty meetings are a part of my job, and I will go and see what I can learn."

RELAXATION TECHNIQUES

When I become over-whelmed by my day or if I find myself needing an escape, I use one of the relaxation exercises. My favorite is "Vacation Time."

—Seventh-grade teacher

The three relaxation techniques described in the classroom activities for this module can work wonders, both for you and for your students. "Vacation Time" uses guided imagery to create a safe place and in turn manage stress. "Relaxation Time," based on the principles of progressive relaxation training (Bernstein & Borkovec, 1973) focuses on the role of physical tension in maintaining anger and stress. Finally, "Self-

Calming Technique" involves identifying physical and emotional cues that accompany anger and upset, using stretching and controlled breathing to facilitate relaxation.

These techniques can be used with students on a daily basis, before a big test, or whenever you feel tension beginning to rise in the classroom. These techniques are also appropriate for you. Practiced regularly, they can help calm your mind and relax your body. It may be helpful to read the spoken directions from each activity into a tape recorder. You can then play the tape for your class or listen to it yourself at your leisure.

CONTENT REVIEW

The following statements refer to the learning goals of this module. Take a minute to think about the statements. Ask yourself whether you feel confident that you can say yes to each. If not, take some time to revisit those topics and consider ways to strengthen your learning.

I have taken a close look at all of my stressors and recognize the degree of pressure I am under on a daily basis.	Yes ❑	No ❑
I can recognize when I am becoming frustrated or beginning to think negatively about my work or personal life.	Yes ❑	No ❑
I am doing something special for myself each day (e.g., journaling, exercising, etc.).	Yes ❑	No ❑
I am using my Support Team for comfort, consultation, and problem solving.	Yes ❑	No ❑
I have determined to do my best while I am at school and attempt to leave the frustrations of the school day at work.	Yes ❑	No ❑
I will take control of stressful situations and not allow them to take control of me. I will identify the problem, step back to gain a clear perspective, review the situation, and plan the best way to respond.	Yes ❑	No ❑
I have acknowledged the thoughts, feelings, and behaviors that accompany my stress in order to combat them.	Yes ❑	No ❑
I have identified specific relaxation techniques that I will encourage my students to practice and will incorporate into my own daily routine.	Yes ❑	No ❑

A Reminder . . .

CLASSROOM INTERACTION AND AWARENESS CHART

Use the CIAC to describe any bullying behavior you observe (and that students report to you, if you wish). Specific instructions for filling out the CIAC appear in Appendix D, along with a blank copy of the chart.

THE BIG QUESTIONS

Focus yourself and honestly appraise your progress by asking yourself the "Big Questions." There are no right or wrong answers.

As concerns relaxation for myself and my students:

1. What is my goal?

2. What am I doing?

3. Is what I am doing helping me achieve my goal?

4. *(If not)* What can I do differently?

PERSONAL GOALS FORM

The Personal Goals Form, on the next page, is designed to help you tailor the content of this module to your own students and situation. If you have not filled out the form as you worked through the information component of the module, please take a moment to do so now.

Personal Goals Form

GOALS

- To become aware of stress and its effects
- To acquire knowledge about general ways to manage stress
- To learn steps to manage on-the-job stress
- To learn specific relaxation techniques to reduce stress on a daily basis

1. Reasons it is important to find ways for myself and my students to relax:

   _____

   _____

2. I have identified the following situations in my personal life and/or classroom where relaxation techniques would be helpful:

   _____

   _____

3. I will conduct the following classroom activities to help myself and my students learn ways to relax:

   _____

   _____

4. I will give students feedback on their understanding of relaxation techniques by encouraging classroom discussion of students' experiences using the techniques. *(Please indicate any other means of feedback in the space below.)*

   _____

   _____

5. I will share my experiences in applying the information in this module with members of my Support Team, other teachers, administrators, parents. *(Please specify who and when in the space below.)*

   _____

   _____

Please continue to fill out the Classroom Interaction and Awareness Chart. Under "Interventions," note how relaxation techniques might be applied to help prevent an incident or to intervene after one has occurred.

Classroom Activities

VACATION TIME

In this activity, students create a special "vacation spot." By imagining a peaceful place, they can reduce immediate stress. The technique takes about 2 minutes; it is fun and can be used anywhere, at any time.

RELAXATION TIME

Often people feel tension as it mounts. This activity can be completed in about 5 minutes; it is designed to help students recognize the physical tension that accompanies stress and anger by encouraging them to tense and relax specific muscle groups.

SELF-CALMING TECHNIQUE

This technique helps students become aware of the feelings and physiological responses that accompany anger and upset, and to interrupt the escalation of feelings before problems arise. Once students are able to recognize these feelings and responses, they can use this technique to calm themselves.

Vacation Time

OBJECTIVES

- To help students recognize when they need to take time to reduce their stress level

- To help students learn how to create a safe place to help manage their stress

- To teach students a relaxation exercise that they can use at any time, in any location

MATERIALS

- None

DIRECTIONS

1. Say to the class, "When your day gets stressful or when you find yourself needing a break, do you ever wish you could get away? Today, we will create a safe vacation place that allows you to relax, regardless of where you are."

2. Read the following directions one at a time to your class. Read each slowly, allowing time for students to create the vacation spot in their minds.

   Place your head on your desk.

   Close your eyes.

   Take a deep breathe and exhale, all of the way.

   Imagine a place you love. This can be a favorite place or a place you have never visited.

   Where are you? Are you on a beach? Near water? In the mountains?

   What does your place look like? Is it sunny or dark? Are there flowers or trees? Is there grass, snow, sand, or water?

   Are you by yourself or with others? Who are the other people?

   What are you doing while you are there? Are you basking in the sun? Waterskiing? Reading a book?

   What is the weather like? Is it warm? Chilly? Breezy? Raining?

What does it smell like? Ocean air? Spring flowers? A crisp winter's day?

What do you like most about this place? Just think about it; don't say it aloud.

This is your vacation spot. Engrave this picture into your mind. When you are feeling stressed, angry, or sad, think of your vacation place and visit it. Allow yourself to become relaxed.

Before your vacation is over, take a mental "snapshot" so that you can have a memory of your vacation.

When I count down from 10, I want you to open your eyes. 10, 9, 8, 7, 6, 5, 4, 3, 2, 1. Open your eyes.

3. Process the activity by conducting a class discussion.

DISCUSSION

- What were you feeling and thinking as you did this activity?

- Where do you go when you take a vacation in your mind?

- How specific are you when you take a vacation in your mind? Do you picture the scene, identify the smells, hear the sounds? Or do you relax and just experience a pleasant calmness?

- How might you use this technique outside of class time?

Relaxation Time

OBJECTIVES

- To help students reduce physiological tension by identifying and relaxing muscles that are tense

- To assist students in distinguishing between tension and deep relaxation

MATERIALS

- None

DIRECTIONS

1. Ask the class to position themselves comfortably at their desks or in chairs.

2. Read the following directions, one at a time, to your class. Read slowly, allowing a few seconds pause between each direction:

   Close your eyes.

   Wrinkle your forehead. Hold for 10 seconds. Relax. Repeat.

   Clench your jaw. Hold for 10 seconds. Relax. Repeat.

   Press your lips tightly together. Hold for 10 seconds. Relax. Repeat.

   Raise your shoulders. Hold for 10 seconds. Relax. Repeat.

   Clench your fists. Hold. Relax. Repeat.

   Tighten your arms. Hold. Relax. Repeat.

   Tighten your stomach. Hold. Relax. Repeat.

   Tighten your buttocks. Hold. Relax. Repeat.

   Tighten your thighs. Hold. Relax. Repeat.

   Point your toes. Make your calves tense. Hold. Relax. Repeat.

   Experience the relaxation in your forehead. Relax your eyebrows.

   Loosen your shoulders. Feel the relaxation deepening in your shoulders, arms, and hands.

   Notice the feeling of looseness in your thighs, buttocks, and calves.

   Open your eyes.

3. Conduct a class discussion, using the following questions.

DISCUSSION

- What were you feeling and thinking as you did this activity?

- Have you used a technique like this before? How did it work for you?

- How might you use this technique outside of class time?

Self-Calming Technique

OBJECTIVES

- To help students learn to identify times when they are becoming angry or stressed

- To teach and encourage students to use a self-calming method to help them regain control

MATERIALS

- None

DIRECTIONS

1. Teach students how to calm themselves by practicing the following steps. Read each step slowly and pause between each direction:

   Close your eyes and take a deep breath.

   Think for a moment about this question: When becoming angry, what do you feel at first? Does your heart race? Do you clench your fists? Do you feel like you are losing control? Don't answer aloud; just think about it.

   To help you calm down, I want you to do the following:

   Bend from your waist and hang down. Hold this position for 5 seconds. Now, come up very slowly.

   Swing your shoulders from left to right. Repeat.

   Drop your head down, touching your chin to your chest. Roll your head around gently in a circular motion.

   When all your muscles feel relaxed, slow down your breathing.

   Feel the breathing in your stomach.

   Feel the calmness throughout your body.

2. Process the activity by conducting a class discussion.

DISCUSSION

- What were you feeling and thinking as you did this activity?

- What did you feel like when the activity was over?

- How does this feeling differ from when you first started the activity?

- How might you use this technique outside of class time?

APPENDIX

A Additional Classroom Activities

Changing Leaves

OBJECTIVES

- To allow students to recognize that everyone has characteristics to improve

- To help each student identify an area for self-improvement and evaluate how improvement in this area will affect others

- To help students recognize how they can become healthier individuals

- To facilitate a discussion about the importance of growth and change in individuals

MATERIALS

- Changing Leaves worksheet

- Crayons or colored markers

DIRECTIONS

1. Distribute the Changing Leaves worksheet to each student and instruct each student to complete it.

2. Instruct students to draw several different colored leaves on the Changing Leaves worksheet. Inside each leaf, the students should write one characteristic they would like to improve (e.g., patience, respect, attitude).

3. Invite each student to share with the class one characteristic he or she would like to improve.

4. Process the activity by conducting a class discussion.

DISCUSSION

- Why is it important to identify characteristics you would like to improve?

- How will improving yourself affect others?

- Was it difficult to think of characteristics to improve?

- How did it feel to share a characteristic to improve with the class?

- Do your classmates want to improve similar or different characteristics?

- How can you support your fellow classmates in making improvements?

- Does anyone have other ideas to share to help us achieve our goals?

CHANGING LEAVES

Setting the Stage for Success

OBJECTIVES

- To help students gain insight into the roles of different classmates
- To foster an understanding of the dynamics that occur within the bully/victim interaction
- To empower students to create solutions to the bullying problem

MATERIALS

- The Playwright worksheet
- Chalkboard or easel pad

DIRECTIONS

1. Give each student a copy of The Playwright worksheet. Read or ask a volunteer to read the "Theme" aloud to the class.

2. Invite students to write brief answers to the questions listed under "Setting and Plot."

3. After students have had a chance to jot down their ideas, divide the class into groups of four or five.

4. Invite students to share their play ideas within their groups. Together, group members can create a play that illustrates a bullying dilemma and a positive solution to it. Encourage all group members to play a role: bully, victim, and bystander victim, as well as additional characters.

5. Have the groups perform their plays for the class. After each play, take a class vote as to whether or not students think the solution depicted would be effective. Tally the votes on the chalkboard or easel pad.

6. Conduct a class discussion, using the following questions.

DISCUSSION

- What play appeared to have the most successful resolution to bullying? Why?

- Are there many or few means to help stop bullying?

- What ideas would not work to stop the bullying?

- How can you use these positive solutions to intervene in bullying you are witnessing or experiencing?

- What was it like to be the bully in the play? The victim? The bystander?

THE PLAYWRIGHT

THEME

A group of characters are being victimized by a group of bullies throughout the school year. Many students stand back and watch this bullying continue because they are afraid to take a stand against the bullies. However, one group of students decides to join with the victim group and solve the bullying dilemma. Together, they succeed in solving the problem.

SETTING AND PLOT

➢ Where does the bullying occur?

➢ When does it happen?

➢ What happens between the bully and the victim?

➢ What do the bystanders and other individuals do to help stop the bullying or keep it from happening in the first place?

➢ How do the bullies and victims react to the other individuals when they try to help?

CHARACTERS

Roles   **Played by**

World Fair

OBJECTIVES

- To increase understanding of each student's cultural heritage

- To facilitate appreciation of cultural diversity

- To create an accepting environment where each student can be valued for his or her unique contributions

MATERIALS

- A few days before conducting this activity, inform the class that they are going to organize a "world fair." The purpose of this fair is to introduce the class to different cultures. Instruct each student to collect stories and traditions from their families. In addition, they can bring in drawings, tokens, pictures, music, and/or food to share with the class.

DIRECTIONS

1. Move the students' desks into a large circle.

2. Have students display, on their desks, the items they have chosen to reflect their family's cultural heritage.

3. After students have had a chance to walk around and observe the "exhibits," have them take their seats. Go around the circle and ask each student to share a special family story or explain the item to the class.

4. Process the activity by conducting a class discussion.

DISCUSSION

- What did you learn from the different exhibits?

- How are the exhibits the same? How are they different?

- What new information did you learn about your classmates?

- What do you want to learn more about?

- How does gaining information about a person's cultural heritage help you to understand that person better?

Day in the Life

OBJECTIVES

- To help students understand how their peers spend their days
- To help students experience what it is like to live the life of a classmate
- To encourage students to recognize the diversity and variation in other students' daily lives

MATERIALS

- Day in the Life worksheet

DIRECTIONS

1. Give students a copy of the Day in the Life worksheet and have them complete it individually.

2. Have the class count off in groups of three. If there appear to be close friends in any group, switch them into another group to provide them with the opportunity of talking with new people.

3. Allow group members to share their answers.

4. Conduct a class discussion, using the following questions.

DISCUSSION

- Have you ever thought about your classmates' days and what they do?
- What surprised you?
- What things do you and other members of your group have in common? What things are different?
- What do you understand now about your classmates that you did not know previously?

DAY IN THE LIFE

1   When do you wake up? Does anyone wake you up?

2   What do you have for breakfast?

3   How do you get to school?

4   Do you go to school with anyone else? If so, whom?

5   How do you feel about going to school in the morning?

6   Do you have friends that you look forward to seeing at school?

7   How do other students treat you throughout the day? At lunch? At recess?

8   How do your teachers treat you?

9   What subjects do you like? What subjects don't you like?

10   Are you afraid of anything or anyone while you are at school?

11   How do you get home? Who is at home when you arrive?

12   What do you like to do after school?

13   Do you play? If so, with whom?

14   Do you have homework? Do you do it?

15   What is dinner like for you at your house?

16   Do you have any favorite evening activities? Shows? Games? Music?

17   When do you go to sleep?

Story Time

OBJECTIVES

- To help students recognize and identify the feelings of others
- To allow students to discuss motivations and actions of fictional characters

MATERIALS

- A work of fiction that students have already been assigned to read or one relevant to your course of academic study

DIRECTIONS

1. Read the book to the class or assign sections of the book as homework.
2. After students have read the material, allow them to identify the main characters.
3. Create a list of each character's traits or characteristics: sensitive, humorous, angry, and so forth.
4. Identify a dilemma, situation, or interaction that occurred in the story.
5. Conduct a class discussion regarding the characters' actions and possible feelings they experienced.

DISCUSSION

- How did the characters become involved in the situation?
- What roles did the various characters play?
- How and why were the characters involved?
- How did the characters respond to one another in the story?
- What personality characteristics or feelings may have motivated the characters to do what they did?
- Why do you think the characters felt the way they did? How would you feel if you were in the same situation?

- Did outside factors influence the characters' feelings and decisions, such as having a bad day or getting in a fight at home?

- Do you relate to any of the characters in the story? Which ones and why?

- Do you think there were different ways the characters could have responded in this situation? (Discuss other ways of acting and feeling in the same situation.)

- What would you have done in a similar situation?

All Ears

OBJECTIVES

- To help students learn the definition and key components of empathy
- To help students become more active and empathic listeners

MATERIALS

- Teacher's Empathy Educator
- Please Let Me Understand worksheet

DIRECTIONS

1. Discuss the term *empathy* with your students, based on the information given in the Teacher's Empathy Educator, on the next page.

2. Distribute the Please Let Me Understand worksheets, one per student, then divide the class into dyads.

3. Instruct the dyads to read each scenario and brainstorm possible empathic and nonempathic responses.

4. Have the class come together again and share the responses they created.

5. Conduct a class discussion, using the following questions.

DISCUSSION

- How can you tell when someone else is being an empathic listener?
- How can you be an empathic listener?
- What is the difference between an empathic listener and someone who just listens?
- How do you understand how someone else is feeling?
- Do some responses seem to be more understanding than others?
- What makes a good empathic response to someone's story?
- What is it like to feel empathy toward another person and that person's life situation?

TEACHER'S EMPATHY EDUCATOR

The purpose of the following discussion is to provide teachers with knowledge about empathy. The information serves as a guide for teaching students the definition of empathy and the key components in being empathic with others.

DEFINITIONS OF EMPATHY

- The ability to understand how it feels to walk in someone else's shoes

- A level of understanding that allows you to relate closely to how another individual is feeling

- The ability to be a good listener and to understand the issue a person is confiding in you

- The ability to demonstrate to another that you are interested in what that person has to say and that you have a desire to understand his or her position

THE EMPATHIC RESPONSE

A person knows you are empathic by your response to what that person is saying. A genuine, interested response lets the person know you are listening and have the desire to understand his or her story.

Have you ever had the experience of sharing an important story with another individual and having that person dismiss it as unimportant? Or maybe the individual turns and walks away from you? Even worse, the person blames you for the feelings you are experiencing? If this has happened to you, you know what it is like to have someone misunderstand you and neglect your story.

Isn't it nice when someone is truly interested and pays close attention to what you have to say? Isn't it wonderful when you tell someone your situation and the person acknowledges you and recognizes that you are in a really tough spot! This is when you have experienced empathy from another individual.

KEY COMPONENTS OF EMPATHY

- A genuine interest in others, communicated through words or actions

- Desire to understand another individual

- Ability to acknowledge and identify how another person is feeling

- Skills to respond to another individual in a caring and understanding manner

MODELING

As a teacher, your empathic responses to students are crucial. Empathic responses can be difficult for students at times, particularly when they do not know how to relate to a specific situation or person. Therefore, it becomes very important for you to model empathic responses in your interactions with your students. If you respond to students in a judgmental or critical manner, this will give students permission to respond in a similar manner. If you respond in a genuine and empathic way, your students will be able to follow the examples you set.

PLEASE LET ME UNDERSTAND

SCENARIO 1

Karyn is a seventh grader and new at her middle school. Although she had close friends at her old school, she hasn't made many friends at her new school. She walks to class by herself, eats lunch by herself, and stands alone at recess. Karyn has overheard some boys call her a "freak." You also heard the boys make this comment and see Karyn standing by herself.

Karyn may feel:

A nonempathic response would be:

An empathic response would be:

SCENARIO 2

Fredrick is the one of the smallest boys in the eighth grade. He really wants to fit in with the other kids, but he is often excluded from their conversations and games during the school day. Therefore, Fredrick often stays by himself or with his one friend. As Fredrick was walking down the hallway, he tripped on his shoelace. When he fell to the ground, his books flew in every direction. The worst part for Fredrick was that he tripped right in front of Torrence, who always makes fun of him for being a "nerd." You were also in the hallway and saw Fredrick trip.

Fredrick may feel:

A nonempathic response would be:

An empathic response would be:

Appendix A: Additional Classroom Activities

Classroom Wish List

OBJECTIVES

- To allow students to voice their ideas for creating a comfortable and safe classroom environment
- To allow students to identify means of improving the classroom for success in academics and interpersonal relations

MATERIALS

- My Wish List worksheet

DIRECTIONS

1. Distribute copies of the My Wish List worksheet, one per student.

2. Instruct students to write down three wishes they would like to have granted to make their classroom a better place.

3. Allow each student to name the number-one wish on his or her list for classroom improvement.

4. Process the activity by conducting a class discussion.

DISCUSSION

- Why did you select these three particular wishes?
- Do other students have similar wishes for the classroom?
- *(If a common wish is identified)* Why do you believe this is important to the success of the classroom?
- What would the classroom be like if all the wishes came true?
- What wishes is it most important to grant?

MY WISH LIST

If I could have anything I wanted to make my classroom a safer and more comfortable place, it would be:

1

2

3

Jump into My Shoes

OBJECTIVES

- To help students understand what it feels like to be a victim of bullying

- To encourage students to be able to take the perspective of the victim to further understand that person's needs

- To allow students to gain the skills and insight to take another individual's perspective

MATERIALS

- Chalkboard or easel pad

DIRECTIONS

PART I

1. Create two columns on the chalkboard or easel pad, labeled "bully" and "victim."

2. Discuss with the class feelings associated with being a bully and being a victim. Ask the students what types of physical reactions each would have. What words would they say to one another? What would each be thinking? How would each feel?

3. When a characteristic is identified, write it in the appropriate column.

4. Select two students to role-play a bully/victim interaction using the characteristics identified through the class discussion. Also divide the classroom in two: Half will support the bully, and half will support the victim.

5. After the role-play, conduct a class discussion, using the questions at the end of the activity.

PART II

1. Allow the role-players to switch positions. The previous bully becomes the victim in a new role-play.

2. Ask the previous bully, and the half of the classroom supporting him or her, how it feels to be in the position of victim. How is it dif-

ferent? Encourage the class to discuss what it is like to be the victim.

3. Ask the previous victim and the victim supporters what it feels like to have their feelings understood by the bully and his or her supporters. Does it make a difference? Do they think this will help the bully and bully supporters think about the victim's perspective? What else should they know and be aware of in their future interactions?

DISCUSSION

- (To students in the role-play) How did you feel about your position? What did it feel like to be the bully? The victim?

- (To the class) Would you want to be in either position? Why or why not?

- What did you think of the bully and the victim?

- How did you feel observing this interaction?

- Did you see any actions or experience any feelings you have not previously? If so, what were they?

Communication Connections

OBJECTIVES

- To encourage recognition that what we say to others has an impact on them
- To aid students in understanding that what we mean to say is not always communicated clearly to another person
- To help students identify the intent and impact of their communication
- To help students understand when a miscommunication has occurred

MATERIALS

- Communication Connections worksheet
- Chalkboard or easel pad

DIRECTIONS

1. Distribute the Communication Connections worksheet, one per student, and have each student complete the worksheet individually.
2. Allow students to share their responses with the class. Write students' responses on the chalkboard or easel pad as they generate them.
3. Process the activity by conducting a class discussion.

DISCUSSION

- Have you ever said something and had someone take it the wrong way?
- What does it feel like to have your words misunderstood?
- What does the phrase "Actions speak louder than words" mean?
- Do you say things to others that can be hurtful without thinking about what you are saying?
- Have you ever wanted to give feedback but feared it would impact the person negatively—for example, make the person mad?

- How can you be more aware of the effects of your words and actions on others?

- How can you correct a situation in which you believe someone else has misunderstood what you were trying to say?

COMMUNICATION CONNECTIONS

1 Your feelings were hurt by one of your friends, although he or she doesn't know it. What can you do to address the situation?

2 A classmate has really been getting on your nerves lately. You want to talk about it, but you are afraid he or she will get mad at you or you will hurt the person's feelings. How can you communicate your feelings effectively and end the conflict?

3 Although you don't know James very well, you just don't like him. You don't talk to him and hardly look at him. When you do look at him, you just roll your eyes. James confronts you and asks you what the problem is. You respond that there is no problem and that you don't even talk to him. How did James know you didn't like him? Did you want James to know this?

4 When Kevin and Sanjay get in an argument, it always ends in a physical fight. Although neither of them likes to fight, they just don't seem to be able to communicate effectively with each other. Out of frustration, they begin to punch and kick. How can Kevin and Sanjay communicate their feelings effectively without fighting and then getting in trouble?

5 Monica always has lots to say. She tends to have many opinions and isn't afraid to share them with anyone who will listen. Sometimes her words are hurtful to others. You have decided to keep all of your opinions to yourself because you don't want to be like Monica and hurt anyone's feelings. How can you communicate your opinions without hurting someone else?

6 You are a great comedian, and your classmates think you are really funny. Sometimes you tell jokes you heard, and sometimes you tell jokes about other people. One day, when you told a joke about Jason's new haircut, everyone started to laugh, but you noticed Jason got up and left the room. You realized at that moment that you hurt Jason's feelings and it is not appropriate to tell jokes about another person. How can you apologize to Jason and share with him that you knew you shouldn't have made fun of him?

7 Lola is an acquaintance. She seems nice enough to you, but sometimes you are not sure you understand what she is saying to you. Today, she walked up to you and commented on your answer to a question the teacher asked in history class. You are unsure how to take her comment. What can you do to clear up the confusion you are experiencing?

Ouch! That Hurt

OBJECTIVES

- To help students recognize that every person makes mistakes and, although mistakes are not good, one can make attempts to mend the situation

- To promote the ability to accept responsibility for actions and make a commitment to improve behavior

- To assist students in discovering multiple ways of apologizing in a difficult situation

MATERIALS

- Ouch! That Hurt worksheet

DIRECTIONS

1. Distribute a copy of the Ouch! That Hurt worksheet to each student.

2. Divide the class into dyads. Provide approximately 10 to 15 minutes for students to complete their worksheets jointly.

3. Bring the class together in a circle.

4. Conduct a class discussion, using the following questions.

DISCUSSION

- What is the purpose of an apology?

- Do you find it difficult to apologize?

- Are some situations harder than others?

- Has someone ever apologized to you? How did it feel?

- Does it make a difference in how you feel if someone genuinely apologizes to you?

- Do you ever feel that you don't owe someone an apology, even if you have hurt the person?

OUCH! THAT HURT

SCENARIO 1

Larry told Marcus that Tybias called Marcus a punk. Marcus thought he would really get Tybias back for disrespecting him in this way. Marcus decided that he would get him back by telling a secret that Tybias had confided about one of his family members. Marcus told everyone he knew the secret. Larry approached Marcus and confessed he was just kidding about what Tybias said and couldn't believe Marcus took it so seriously. Later in the afternoon, Marcus found Tybias crouched in the corner of the bathroom in complete sadness and embarrassment.

How can Marcus apologize?

What can Marcus do to prevent this situation from occurring again?

SCENARIO 2

Ashley was so tired of Melonie's always bragging about the new clothes and jewelry she was buying. Ashley didn't have much money and was jealous of Melonie's extravagant lifestyle. One afternoon during gym class, Ashley stole Melonie's watch from her locker. Ashley felt guilty, but she also felt it served Melonie right. After gym class, Melonie realized her watch was gone and began to cry because the watch was given to her by her grandmother. Ashley recognized she was wrong and wanted to give the watch back.

How can Ashley apologize?

What can Ashley do to take responsibility for her behavior and prevent the situation from reoccurring?

SCENARIO 3

Kevin is one of the smallest kids in the class and is often bullied by other students, particularly Andy. One day, Andy was in a really aggressive mood and began to beat up Kevin. Andy had been working hard on improving his behavior and not being a bully, but this day he lost control.

How can Andy apologize to Kevin?

How can Andy take responsibility for his behavior and not blame it on Kevin?

Firm Foundations

OBJECTIVES

- To help students clarify beliefs and values about peer pressure and bullying
- To identify how students want others to perceive them
- To increase students' awareness of how they can express their values to improve their school community

MATERIALS

- "Firm Foundations" worksheet

DIRECTIONS

1. Give each student a copy of the Firm Foundations worksheet. Have students complete their worksheets independently.

2. Allow students to move their desks into a circle or to sit in a circle. Encourage each student to read his or her responses to the group.

3. Create a space on the wall or bulletin board to display students' Firm Foundations worksheets as a continual reminder of their values and beliefs.

4. Process the activity by conducting a class discussion.

DISCUSSION

- What values are commonly shared among the class?
- How do others know what you believe and stand for?
- How can you take action and contribute positively to the school community?
- What happens when someone does not respect your values?
- Do you ever see people with values that you don't respect? What are these values? What do you do when this happens?

FIRM FOUNDATIONS

*My values are the foundation for my
thoughts and actions.*

The characteristics I value in myself are . . .

People can see that I hold these values because I . . .

In order to make our school community a place
where our positive values are respected, I can . . .

Classroom Rights Amendment

OBJECTIVES

- To encourage students to collaborate to identify rights deserved by all
- To help all students participate actively in determining the classroom atmosphere
- To create a document stating the basic needs and privileges due every student

MATERIALS

- Declaration of Classroom Rights
- Chalkboard or easel pad
- Posterboard and markers

DIRECTIONS

1. Divide the class into groups of three to four students each. Give each group a Declaration of Classroom Rights.

2. Allow 10 to 15 minutes for group discussion on what students believe to be the given rights of all students.

3. Reconvene in the larger group. Encourage each small group to share the rights they identified.

4. Write each group's suggestions on the chalkboard or easel pad to create a comprehensive list of rights considered important by all students. As the teacher, you can add values you believe are essential if students do not name them.

5. Conduct a class discussion, using the following questions. Following discussion, create or have students create a bulletin board or poster to display the list of classroom rights to be observed by all.

DISCUSSION

- Why are these rights important?

- Did the different groups come up with many of the same rights? Different rights?

- What happens when someone's rights are violated?

- What do you do when you observe someone else's rights being violated?

- How do you feel when your rights are violated? How do you react?

DECLARATION OF CLASSROOM RIGHTS

We believe all students in this class should hereby be granted the following rights:

_____

_____

_____

_____

_____

_____

_____

_____

_____

_____

_____

_____

_____

_____

_____

_____

_____

_____

_____

_____

Appendix A: Additional Classroom Activities

I Believe

OBJECTIVES

- To allow students to clarify their beliefs regarding bullying
- To help students recognize the diversity of beliefs among their peers
- To give students the opportunity to announce their beliefs publicly to their classmates

MATERIALS

- I Believe worksheet

DIRECTIONS

1. Distribute the I Believe worksheets, one per student. Allow students to complete their worksheets individually.

2. When students have completed their worksheets, ask them to stand up and form a single line across the room.

3. Read each item aloud, one at a time. Instruct the students to move according to their answers as follows:

   True: Take two steps FORWARD.

   False: Take two steps BACKWARD.

   Undecided: Remain in place.

4. Process the activity by conducting a class discussion.

DISCUSSION

- Were some questions easier to answer than others?
- Which questions were particularly difficult to answer?
- Could one of your classmates persuade you to change any of your responses, positively or negatively?
- Are any of your responses influenced by experiences you have had or observed?
- Did some people in the group answer differently from the way you thought they would?

- Is it acceptable if you and a close friend or someone you respect answered an item differently?

- What would happen in a situation where two people were friends but held different values concerning an activity or behavior?

I Believe

Instructions: Circle your response to each item.

1. It is better to go along with my friends than to defend my own beliefs.

   TRUE   **UNDECIDED**   **FALSE**

2. Some people deserve to be bullied because of their looks or behaviors.

   TRUE   **UNDECIDED**   **FALSE**

3. If someone starts a fight with me, my only option is to fight them back in order to defend myself and my reputation.

   TRUE   **UNDECIDED**   **FALSE**

4. I like only people who are similar to me and who hold the same beliefs I do.

   TRUE   **UNDECIDED**   **FALSE**

5. When I hear a rumor about someone, I am likely to believe it.

   TRUE   **UNDECIDED**   **FALSE**

6. When people are gossiping, I am likely to join them and pass the information along to others.

   TRUE   **UNDECIDED**   **FALSE**

7. I believe it is OK to recognize when I purposely or accidentally hurt someone and to take action to correct myself and the situation.

   TRUE   **UNDECIDED**   **FALSE**

8. If someone is being bullied, I believe I have the ability to help stop the bullying interaction.

   TRUE   **UNDECIDED**   **FALSE**

Lend a Hand

OBJECTIVES

- To increase students' abilities to recognize when someone needs their help

- To increase students' comfort level with helping someone voluntarily

- To encourage students to ask for someone else's help when a situation is too big for them

- To teach students how to respond if someone rejects their offer to help

MATERIALS

- Lend a Hand worksheet

DIRECTIONS

1. Distribute the Lend a Hand worksheets, one copy per student.

2. Divide the class into groups of three to four students each. Allow students to read and discuss their options for each scenario.

3. Bring the class back together in a circle. Ask students to raise their hands if they find offering help challenging. Ask students to raise their hands if they are comfortable and willing to offer help to others. Encourage students to discuss their responses

4. Process the activity by conducting a class discussion.

DISCUSSION

- How do you recognize when someone is in need of help?

- If you aren't able to assist, what do you do?

- Have you ever offered to help someone, and the person responded negatively? Why do you think the person responded this way?

- Has someone offered you help when you needed it?

- Was there ever a time you needed help and didn't get it? How did you feel?

- Do you ever want to help and don't? Why or why not?

LEND A HAND

SCENARIO 1

Troy was walking down the hall when Bart tripped him. Troy fell to the ground, and his books flew in every direction. A few people began to giggle and call Troy a klutz. You are not close friends with Troy; however, you notice he looks very embarrassed.

How can you be of help?

What do you do?

SCENARIO 2

Sara, Mika, and Lola cornered Cyndi in the bathroom. They were accusing her of liking Mika's boyfriend. Cyndi told them she didn't even know him. Together, the girls began to yell at Cyndi, and finally Mika pushed her to the ground. You walk in just at this moment.

How can you be of help?

What do you do?

SCENARIO 3

Bill and Edward are scary. Everyone knows it and stays as far away as possible from them. They like this because it makes them feel powerful. You are really tired of their acting like they own the whole school. As you walk into the cafeteria, you see them knock Steve's food tray to the ground.

How can you be of help?

What do you do?

SCENARIO 4

Every day on your way to the bus stop, you observe a group of older boys and girls harassing younger kids. They call the younger kids names and take their lunches or lunch money. Each day you walk with your head down and hope they don't notice you. Although they don't notice you, you realize what these younger kids are going through.

How can you be of help?

What do you do?

Thanks a Bunch

OBJECTIVES

- To help students recognize when they are thankful
- To encourage students to express their appreciation to others

MATERIALS

- Thanks a Bunch worksheet
- Chalkboard or easel pad

DIRECTIONS

1. Give each student a copy of the Thanks a Bunch worksheet. Allow students to complete the worksheets independently.

2. Divide the class into groups of four to five students each. Instruct group members to share their responses with one another. Encourage them to brainstorm creative ways of expressing their appreciation in each scenario.

3. Reconvene in the larger group, and allow each small group to share their creative responses. Write their responses on the chalkboard or easel pad.

4. Conduct a class discussion, using the following questions.

DISCUSSION

- What is the purpose of showing appreciation?
- Were there any items that you felt did not deserve a thank-you? Why or why not?
- Is it easy to show appreciation to others?
- If you don't like someone, are you less likely to say thank you? If so, why?
- How do you feel when someone thanks you?
- Is it ever challenging to accept someone's thanks or appreciation?
- Is it easier to give or to receive thanks?

THANKS A BUNCH

Instructions: For each action, do you think a thank-you would be appropriate? If so, please write how you can you show your appreciation. If you would not appreciate the action, please explain how would you respond.

1 Your parent or guardian packed your lunch for school.

2 A person in your class told you that your artwork was incredible.

3 A person you don't like did something nice for you.

4 A person from the community came to speak to your class about school violence.

5 A classmate told another classmate to stop picking on you.

6 A classmate you hardly know told you he/she admired your strength in gym class.

7 When your books fell on the ground, someone helped you pick them up.

8 An older student confronted a classmate who had said something rude to you.

9 A person you think is nerdy gave you a compliment.

10 A neighbor gave you a ride to school.

11 Your teacher didn't give you any homework.

12 A classmate brought in candy for the whole class.

APPENDIX

B Teacher Inventory of Skills and Knowledge

This appendix includes the TISK, short for the Teacher Inventory of Skills and Knowledge. Drawn from the seven program modules, the items in the TISK are grouped according to six different categories:

1. Prevention of bullying and victimization

2. Interventions for bullies

3. Interventions for victims

4. Interventions for bullies and victims

5. Resources for bullying and victimization

6. Awareness of bullying and victimization

Each item allows a response on two dimensions: *knowledge* (how knowledgeable you are about a specific skill) and *use* (how often you use the skill).

We encourage you to photocopy and complete the TISK before beginning your study of the program modules. Doing so will help you in two main ways: First, it will serve as a preview of what lies before you. Many of the items you see may be unfamiliar to you. However, seeing them on the inventory may spark your curiosity to look for them as you progress through the modules. Second, completing the TISK before you begin working with the material will give you a baseline, an idea of where you are in terms of knowledge and skills. Knowing where you are is essential to deciding where you want to go.

We encourage you to complete the inventory again after you have studied the material in all the modules. This will allow you to assess your improvement, as well as show areas that may require review. Teachers have shared that they find the information they gain from the TISK invaluable: It opens their eyes to what they have learned and to the frequency with which they are implementing prevention, intervention, and awareness skills into their classrooms and schools.

Filling out and then scoring the TISK, using the Scoring Menu and Scoring Summary in Appendix C, should take you no more than 15 minutes. You may use the inventory as frequently as you would like. It can be particularly useful to take the TISK periodically after completing the modules to assess your retention of skills and knowledge, as well as to refocus your efforts toward change.

Teacher Inventory of Skills and Knowledge (TISK)

Name _____ Date _____

TISK version (how many times have you completed the TISK?) **1 2 3 4 5 6 7 8 9 10**

The following questions concern your knowledge of various interventions for bullies and victims and how often you use certain techniques and resources. Please complete every item by circling the response that most closely reflects (a) your *knowledge* of the intervention and (b) your *use* of the intervention. Blank spaces are provided at the end of the questionnaire for you to list other strategies and resources you have used. *Note:* Items marked with an asterisk (*) are common to teacher training and not unique to a bully prevention program.

Knowledge of the Intervention   **U** = Unfamiliar   **S** = Somewhat familiar   **V** = Very familiar

Use of the Intervention   **N** = Never   **S** = Sometimes   **O** = Often

Intervention	**Knowledge**	**Use**
1. Establish a zero-tolerance policy: "No bullying."	U S V	N S O
2. Teach victims social skills (e.g., self-presentation, nonvictim body language, skills to deal with conflicts).	U S V	N S O
3. Teach victims physical and verbal assertiveness skills (e.g., assertive words, posture, eye contact).	U S V	N S O
4. Use peer mediation (train team of students to help bully and victim work out an agreement).	U S V	N S O
5. Use teacher support team as a resource for consultation and support for bullying problems.	U S V	N S O
6. Use student support team as a resource for consultation and support for bullying problems.	U S V	N S O
7. Use consequences for undesirable acts/misbehavior committed by bullies.	U S V	N S O
8. Reinforce nonbullying behaviors (e.g., on-task behavior, helping behavior, assertive/nonaggressive behavior).	U S V	N S O
9. Teach social skills for entering groups, conversations, and other social activities.	U S V	N S O
10. Teach steps of problem solving and decision making for behavior problems.	U S V	N S O
11. Assist victims of bullying in identifying skills and behaviors they may want to learn.	U S V	N S O

12. Teach confidence and self-esteem building skills to victims.	**U**	**S**	**V**	**N**	**S**	**O**
13. Highlight strengths of victim and bully (help students become aware of their strengths).	**U**	**S**	**V**	**N**	**S**	**O**
14. Use the "Four R's" of bully control: Recognize, Remove, Review, Respond.	**U**	**S**	**V**	**N**	**S**	**O**
15. Instill an attitude of hope and encouragement in bullies and victims.	**U**	**S**	**V**	**N**	**S**	**O**
16. Encourage bullies to understand the victim's point of view (help bullies develop an empathic understanding of victims).	**U**	**S**	**V**	**N**	**S**	**O**
17. Conduct open discussions with bully and victim.	**U**	**S**	**V**	**N**	**S**	**O**
18. Teach bullies to list and prioritize behaviors that need to be changed.	**U**	**S**	**V**	**N**	**S**	**O**
19. Use written contracts with bullies.	**U**	**S**	**V**	**N**	**S**	**O**
20. Use written contracts with victims.	**U**	**S**	**V**	**N**	**S**	**O**
21. Reward for improvements (successive approximations of desired behavior).	**U**	**S**	**V**	**N**	**S**	**O**
22. Teach bullies nonaggressive and nonbullying behavioral alternatives.	**U**	**S**	**V**	**N**	**S**	**O**
23. Teach coping skills to victims.	**U**	**S**	**V**	**N**	**S**	**O**
24. Provide support for victims (create an "open door" policy).	**U**	**S**	**V**	**N**	**S**	**O**
25. Teach bullies a better way of thinking (to shift from aggressive-based appraisals to assertive-based ones).	**U**	**S**	**V**	**N**	**S**	**O**
26. Teach students to recognize and identify the characteristics and behaviors of different types of bullies.	**U**	**S**	**V**	**N**	**S**	**O**
27. Teach students to recognize and identify the characteristics and behaviors of different types of victims.	**U**	**S**	**V**	**N**	**S**	**O**
28. Use an invitational approach (encourage bully and victim to share their perspectives).	**U**	**S**	**V**	**N**	**S**	**O**
29. Reinforce behavior, not the child (e.g., "Bob, I am proud of you for _____").	**U**	**S**	**V**	**N**	**S**	**O**
30. Use praise and attention to reinforce good behaviors and accomplishments.	**U**	**S**	**V**	**N**	**S**	**O**
31. Use the technique of overcorrection with bullies.	**U**	**S**	**V**	**N**	**S**	**O**
32. Use loss of privileges with bullies.	**U**	**S**	**V**	**N**	**S**	**O**
33. Teach all students the lasting effects of victimization.	**U**	**S**	**V**	**N**	**S**	**O**

34. Use role-plays and role reversal to teach bullies what it feels like to be the victim.　　U　S　V　　　N　S　O

35. Conduct follow-up on bullying incidents.　　U　S　V　　　N　S　O

36. Use the empty chair exercise to help students understand the behaviors, thoughts, and feelings of the bully and victim.　　U　S　V　　　N　S　O

*37. Establish and implement classroom rules and a code of conduct.　　U　S　V　　　N　S　O

*38. Model decision making, respect for others, and a positive attitude.　　U　S　V　　　N　S　O

39. Use cooperative learning with bullies and victims (incorporate group projects/team approach into your curriculum).　　U　S　V　　　N　S　O

40. Teach bullies and victims verbal and nonverbal communication skills (e.g., sharing opinions, communicating in situations involving conflict, listening to others).　　U　S　V　　　N　S　O

41. Teach collaborative conflict resolution skills to bullies and victims (teach bullies and victims to become responsible for finding their own solutions through negotiation).　　U　S　V　　　N　S　O

42. Create opportunities for student success.　　U　S　V　　　N　S　O

43. Implement a buddy system (pair reliable student with incoming student).　　U　S　V　　　N　S　O

44. Defuse bullying situations in the classroom immediately and address the issue with the bully after class, privately.　　U　S　V　　　N　S　O

45. Teach anger management strategies to bullies.　　U　S　V　　　N　S　O

46. Teach relaxation techniques to bullies and victims.　　U　S　V　　　N　S　O

47. Teach self-calming techniques to bullies.　　U　S　V　　　N　S　O

48. Teach victims to find their "safe vacation place."　　U　S　V　　　N　S　O

*49. Make a referral to counselor.　　U　S　V　　　N　S　O

*50. Consult with school counselor, school psychologist, or other professional.　　U　S　V　　　N　S　O

51. Verbally correct/reprimand the bully individually to avoid reinforcing attention-seeking behavior.　　U　S　V　　　N　S　O

52. Implement classroom activities to increase awareness of bullying/victimization.　　U　S　V　　　N　S　O

53. Implement classroom activities aimed at bully prevention.　　U　S　V　　　N　S　O

---

54. Use group problem solving for and with other teachers. **U S V   N S O**

55. Have students keep a log of the incidents of bullying/victimization they witness. **U S V   N S O**

*56. Make a disciplinary referral. **U S V   N S O**

57. Contact parents regarding student misbehavior via phone call, letter, conference. **U S V   N S O**

58. Contact parents regarding positive behavior of all students. **U S V   N S O**

59. Teacher/school provides workshops, seminars, and other opportunities for parents to seek new information and skills. **U S V   N S O**

*60. Consult with another teacher for advice. **U S V   N S O**

*61. Use behavior log (record bullying incidents and interventions). **U S V   N S O**

62. Use a consistent signal to indicate that the day's lesson is commencing. **U S V   N S O**

63. Develop a special relationship with each child. **U S V   N S O**

64. Believe that you can successfully bring about a desired outcome in your students (teacher self-efficacy). **U S V   N S O**

Other strategies and resources:

_____   **U S V   N S O**

_____

_____   **U S V   N S O**

_____

_____   **U S V   N S O**

_____

_____   **U S V   N S O**

_____

APPENDIX

C | Scoring the Teacher Inventory of Skills and Knowledge

To score the Teacher Inventory of Skills and Knowledge, photocopy and record your responses for each TISK item on the following Scoring Menu. For instance, if your responses to Item 1 were Somewhat Knowledgeable and Never Use, you would circle *S* for knowledge and *N* for use under the category "Prevention of Bullying and Victimization." After circling your responses for all items, total the number of *U's, S's* and *V's* for the knowledge dimension and the number of *N's , S's* and *O's* for the use dimension, then write each total in the box provided. Next transfer your category totals to the Scoring Summary, given on page 247.

Compare your Scoring Summaries each time you take the TISK. Doing so can provide you with a general idea of your acquisition and retention of knowledge, as well as your use of prevention and intervention strategies. If after having completed the modules you responded Unfamiliar (U) or Somewhat Familiar (S) to a majority of items on the knowledge dimension, you will want to take time to revisit the material associated with those items.

Looking at your responses on the use dimension can give you a picture of how you are implementing different intervention strategies in your work. If you responded Never Use (N) or Sometimes Use (S) to many of the items, take time to start practicing these strategies in your classroom. You can also monitor the balance between prevention and intervention in the strategies you are using at any given time. To do so, compare your responses on the use dimension between the category "Prevention of Bullying and Victimization" and the categories "Interventions for Bullies" and "Interventions for Victims." Which are you using more often, prevention strategies or intervention techniques? If your responses suggest you are using mostly interventions, you may want to reconsider your approach. Remember, prevention is always better than intervention.

If you responded that you are Very Familiar (V) with many of the knowledge items and Often Use (O) a variety of techniques, good for you! You are well on your way toward a safer and more effective classroom and school.

Scoring Menu: Teacher Inventory of Skills and Knowledge

Name _____ Date _____

TISK version (how many times have you completed the TISK?) **1 2 3 4 5 6 7 8 9 10**

Note: Items marked with an asterisk (*) are common to teacher training and not unique to a bully prevention program.

Category	Knowledge	Use
PREVENTION OF BULLYING AND VICTIMIZATION		
1. Establish a zero-tolerance policy: "No bullying."	U S V	N S O
8. Reinforce nonbullying behaviors (e.g., on-task behavior, helping behavior, assertive/nonaggressive behavior).	U S V	N S O
9. Teach social skills for entering groups, conversations, and other social activities.	U S V	N S O
10. Teach steps of problem solving and decision making for behavior problems.	U S V	N S O
13. Highlight strengths of victim and bully (help students become aware of their strengths).	U S V	N S O
29. Reinforce behavior, not the child (e.g., "Bob, I am proud of you for _____").	U S V	N S O
30. Use praise and attention to reinforce good behaviors and accomplishments.	U S V	N S O
*37. Establish and implement classroom rules and a code of conduct.	U S V	N S O
*38. Model decision making, respect for others, and a positive attitude.	U S V	N S O
42. Create opportunities for student success.	U S V	N S O
43. Implement a buddy system (pair reliable student with incoming student).	U S V	N S O
58. Contact parents regarding positive behavior of all students.	U S V	N S O
62. Use a consistent signal to indicate that the day's lesson is commencing.	U S V	N S O

63. Develop a special relationship with each child.   **U S V**   **N S O**

64. Believe that you can successfully bring about a desired outcome in your students (teacher self-efficacy).   **U S V**   **N S O**

TOTAL RESPONSES (U's, S's, V's / N's, S's, O's)
Total the responses and write the number in the box.

☐☐☐   ☐☐☐
U S V   **N S O**

INTERVENTIONS FOR BULLIES

7. Use consequences for undesirable acts/misbehavior committed by bullies.   **U S V**   **N S O**

16. Encourage bullies to understand the victim's point of view (help bullies develop an empathic understanding of victims).   **U S V**   **N S O**

18. Teach bullies to list and prioritize behaviors that need to be changed.   **U S V**   **N S O**

19. Use written contracts with bullies.   **U S V**   **N S O**

22. Teach bullies nonaggressive and nonbullying behavioral alternatives.   **U S V**   **N S O**

25. Teach bullies a better way of thinking (to shift from aggressive-based appraisals to assertive-based ones).   **U S V**   **N S O**

31. Use the technique of overcorrection with bullies.   **U S V**   **N S O**

32. Use loss of privileges with bullies.   **U S V**   **N S O**

34. Use role-plays and role reversal to teach bullies what it feels like to be the victim.   **U S V**   **N S O**

44. Defuse bullying situations in the classroom immediately and address the issue with the bully after class, privately.   **U S V**   **N S O**

45. Teach anger management strategies to bullies.   **U S V**   **N S O**

47. Teach self-calming techniques to bullies.   **U S V**   **N S O**

51. Verbally correct/reprimand the bully individually to avoid reinforcing attention-seeking behavior.   **U S V**   **N S O**

57. Contact parents regarding student misbehavior via phone call, letter, conference.   **U S V**   **N S O**

*61. Use behavior log (record bullying incidents and interventions).   **U S V**   **N S O**

TOTAL RESPONSES (U's, S's, V's / N's, S's, O's)
Total the responses and write the number in the box.

☐☐☐   ☐☐☐
U S V   **N S O**

INTERVENTIONS FOR VICTIMS

			U	S	V		N	S	O
2.	Teach victims social skills (e.g., self-presentation, nonvictim body language, skills to deal with conflicts).		U	S	V		N	S	O
3.	Teach victims physical and verbal assertiveness skills (e.g., assertive words, posture, eye contact).		U	S	V		N	S	O
11.	Assist victims of bullying in identifying skills and behaviors they may want to learn.		U	S	V		N	S	O
12.	Teach confidence and self-esteem building skills to victims.		U	S	V		N	S	O
20.	Use written contracts with victims.		U	S	V		N	S	O
23.	Teach coping skills to victims.		U	S	V		N	S	O
24.	Provide support for victims (create an "open door" policy).		U	S	V		N	S	O
48.	Teach victims to find their "safe vacation place."		U	S	V		N	S	O

TOTAL RESPONSES (U's, S's, V's / N's, S's, O's)
Total the responses and write the number in the box.

☐ ☐ ☐   ☐ ☐ ☐
U S V   N S O

INTERVENTIONS FOR BULLIES AND VICTIMS

4.	Use peer mediation (train team of students to help bully and victim work out an agreement).		U	S	V		N	S	O
14.	Use the "Four R's" of bully control: Recognize, Remove, Review, Respond.		U	S	V		N	S	O
15.	Instill an attitude of hope and encouragement in bullies and victims.		U	S	V		N	S	O
17.	Conduct open discussions with bully and victim.		U	S	V		N	S	O
21.	Reward for improvements (successive approximations of desired behavior).		U	S	V		N	S	O
28.	Use an invitational approach (encourage bully and victim to share their perspectives).		U	S	V		N	S	O
35.	Conduct follow-up on bullying incidents.		U	S	V		N	S	O
36.	Use the empty chair exercise to help students understand the behaviors, thoughts, and feelings of the bully and victim.		U	S	V		N	S	O
39.	Use cooperative learning with bullies and victims (incorporate group projects/team approach into your curriculum).		U	S	V		N	S	O
40.	Teach bullies and victims verbal and nonverbal communication skills (e.g., sharing opinions, communicating in situations involving conflict, listening to others).		U	S	V		N	S	O

41. Teach collaborative conflict resolution skills to bullies and victims (teach bullies and victims to become responsible for finding their own solutions through negotiation).　　　　U　S　V　　　N　S　O

46. Teach relaxation techniques to bullies and victims.　　　U　S　V　　　N　S　O

TOTAL RESPONSES (U's, S's, V's / N's, S's, O's)
Total the responses and write the number in the box.
□□□　　□□□
U　S　V　　N　S　O

RESOURCES FOR BULLYING AND VICTIMIZATION

5. Use teacher support team as a resource for consultation and support for bullying problems.　　U　S　V　　　N　S　O

6. Use student support team as a resource for consultation and support for bullying problems.　　U　S　V　　　N　S　O

*49. Make a referral to counselor.　　　U　S　V　　　N　S　O

*50. Consult with school counselor, school psychologist, or other professional.　　　U　S　V　　　N　S　O

54. Use group problem solving for and with other teachers.　　U　S　V　　　N　S　O

*56. Make a disciplinary referral.　　　U　S　V　　　N　S　O

59. Teacher/school provides workshops, seminars, and other opportunities for parents to seek new information and skills.　　U　S　V　　　N　S　O

*60. Consult with another teacher for advice.　　U　S　V　　　N　S　O

TOTAL RESPONSES (U's, S's, V's / N's, S's, O's)
Total the responses and write the number in the box.
□□□　　□□□
U　S　V　　N　S　O

AWARENESS OF BULLYING AND VICTIMIZATION

26. Teach students to recognize and identify the characteristics and behaviors of different types of bullies.　　U　S　V　　　N　S　O

27. Teach students to recognize and identify the characteristics and behaviors of different types of victims.　　U　S　V　　　N　S　O

33. Teach all students the lasting effects of victimization.　　U　S　V　　　N　S　O

52. Implement classroom activities to increase awareness of bullying/victimization.　　U　S　V　　　N　S　O

53. Implement classroom activities aimed at bully prevention.　　U　S　V　　　N　S　O

55. Have students keep a log of the incidents of bullying/victimization they witness.　　U　S　V　　　N　S　O

TOTAL RESPONSES (U's, S's, V's / N's, S's, O's)
Total the responses and write the number in the box.
□□□　　□□□
U　S　V　　N　S　O

Scoring Summary: Teacher Inventory of Skills and Knowledge

Name _____   Date _____

TISK version (how many times have you completed the TISK?)   **1 2 3 4 5 6 7 8 9 10**

Transfer your scores for each category from the TISK scoring menu onto this chart.

Category	**Knowledge**	**Use**
PREVENTION OF BULLYING AND VICTIMIZATION	☐ ☐ ☐ U S V	☐ ☐ ☐ N S O
INTERVENTIONS FOR BULLIES	☐ ☐ ☐ U S V	☐ ☐ ☐ N S O
INTERVENTIONS FOR VICTIMS	☐ ☐ ☐ U S V	☐ ☐ ☐ N S O
INTERVENTIONS FOR BULLIES AND VICTIMS	☐ ☐ ☐ U S V	☐ ☐ ☐ N S O
RESOURCES FOR BULLYING AND VICTIMIZATION	☐ ☐ ☐ U S V	☐ ☐ ☐ N S O
AWARENESS OF BULLYING AND VICTIMIZATION	☐ ☐ ☐ U S V	☐ ☐ ☐ N S O

APPENDIX

D Classroom Interaction and Awareness Chart

The Classroom Interaction and Awareness Chart (CIAC) allows you to keep track of bullying interactions and how you intervene to deal with them. Recording the bullying incidents you observe in your classroom or other places at school is very important. It gives objective data to evaluate the extent of the problem in your school and allows you to see when progress is being made. When you do recognize improvement, you can let your students know: We all like concrete, specific, and timely feedback about our efforts. Tracking will also increase your awareness of the roles each student plays in the classroom and with his or her peer group. Insight into these roles will assist you in tackling the bullying dilemma.

Our experience is that this type of record keeping will take about 15 minutes a day in the beginning, and the time required will decrease as you become more proficient in recognizing problems and recording their occurrence. It is a good idea to keep the chart on your desk so that you can jot down notes about situations as they occur. You can also record incidents at the end of each day if that is more convenient. Your record does not have to be greatly detailed, but it should include enough information so that you will be able to remember even several months in the future what occurred.

CLASSROOM INTERACTION AND AWARENESS CHART

Week of: _____

DATE	LOCATION/TIME	STUDENT(S)	BEHAVIORS	INTERVENTIONS

References and Suggested Readings

Ahmad, Y., & Smith, P. K. (1994). Bullying in schools and the issue of sex differences. In J. Archer (Ed.), *Male violence*. London: Routledge and Kegan Paul.

Arndt, R. (1994). School violence on rise, survey says. *Nation's Cities Weekly, 17,* 1–2.

Arora, C. M. J., & Thompson, D. A. (1987). Defining bullying for a secondary school. *Educational and Child Psychology, 4,* 110–120.

Ashton, P. T., & Webb, R. B. (1986). *Making a difference: Teachers' sense of efficacy and student achievement.* New York: Longman.

Authier, J., Gustafson, K., Guerney, B., & Kasdorff, J. A. (1975). The psychological practitioner as a teacher: A theoretical-historical and practical review. *Counseling Psychologist, 5,* 31–50.

Bandura, A. (1973). *Aggression: A social learning analysis.* Englewood Cliffs, NJ: Prentice Hall.

Bandura, A. (1977). *Social learning theory.* Englewood Cliffs, NJ: Prentice Hall.

Bandura, A. (1986). *Social foundations of thought and action: A social cognitive theory.* Engelwood Cliffs, NJ: Prentice Hall.

Batsche, G. M., & Knoff, H. M. (1994). Bullies and their victims: Understanding a pervasive problem in the schools. *School Psychology Review, 23,* 165–174.

Berman, P., & McLaughlin, M. (1977). *Federal programs supporting educational change: Vol. 2. Factors affecting implementation and continuation.* (ERIC Document Reproduction Service No. ED 159 289)

Bernstein, D. A., & Borkovec, T. D. (1973). *Progressive relaxation training: A manual for the helping professions.* Champaign, IL: Research Press.

Besag, B. (1989). *Bullies and victims in schools: A guide to understanding and management.* United Kingdom: Open University Press.

Boulton, M. J., & Smith, P. K. (1994). Bully/victim problems in middle-school children: Stability, self-perceived competence, peer perceptions, and peer acceptance. *Journal of Developmental Psychology, 12,* 315–329.

Boulton, M. J., & Underwood, K. (1992). Bully/victim problems among middle-school children. *British Journal of Educational Psychology, 62,* 73–87.

Bryne, B. J. (1994a). Bullies and victims in a school setting with reference to some Dublin schools. *Irish Journal of Psychology, 15,* 574–586.

Bryne, B. J. (1994b). *Coping with bullying in schools.* London: Cassell.

Cairnes, R. B., Cairnes, B. D., Neckerman, H. J., Gest, S. D., & Gariepy, J. L. (1988). Social networks and aggressive behavior: Peer support or peer rejection? *Developmental Psychology, 24,* 815–823.

Carnegie Forum on Education and the Economy. (1986). *A nation prepared: Teachers for the 21st century.* New York: Author.

Coie, J. D., Dodge, K. A., & Coppotelli, H. (1982). Dimensions and types of social status: A cross-age perspective. *Developmental Psychology, 18,* 557–570.

Conye, R. K. (1987). *Primary preventative counseling: Empowering people and systems.* Muncie, IN: Accelerated Development.

Cowie, H. (1994). *Cooperation in the multi-ethnic classroom: The impact of cooperative group work on social relationships in middle school students.* London: Dave Fulton Publishers.

Cowie, H., & Sharp, S. (1994). How to tackle bullying through curriculum. In S. Sharp & P. Smith (Eds.), *Tackling bullying in your school: A practical handbook for teachers.* New York: Routledge.

Dembo, M., & Gibson, S. (1985). Teachers' sense of efficacy: An important factor in school improvement. *The Elementary School Journal, 86,* 173–184.

Dodge, K. A., & Coie, J. D. (1987). Social-information-processing factors in reactive and proactive aggression in children's peer groups. *Journal of Personality and Social Psychology, 53,* 1146–1158.

Durlak, J. A., & Wells, A. M. (1997). Primary prevention mental health programs for children and adolescents: A meta-analytic review. *American Journal of Community Psychology, 25,* 115–152.

Elliot, D. (1994). *Youth violence: An overview.* Boulder: The Center for the Study and Prevention of Violence.

Fecser, F. A., Goldstein, A. P., Piechura, K., & Campbell, B. (1996). The psychoeducational classroom: Strategies and skills of successful methods and social/emotional curricula. In J. Nicholas & W. C. Morse (Eds.), *Conflict in the classroom: The education of at-risk and troubled students.* Austin: PRO-ED.

Feshbach, N. D. (1982). Empathy training and the regulation of aggression: Potentialities and limitations. *Academic Psychology Bulletin, 4,* 399–413.

Fleischman, M. J., Horne, A. M., & Arthur, J. L. (1982). *Troubled families: A treatment program.* Champaign, IL: Research Press.

Floyd, N. M. (1985). "Pick on someone your own size": Controlling victimization. *Pointer, 29,* 9–17.

Forehand, R., & Long, N. (1996). *Parenting the strong-willed child.* Chicago: Contemporary Books.

Fried, S., & Fried, P. F. (1996). *Bullies and victims.* New York: Evans & Company.

Garrity, C., Jens, K., Porter, W., Sayger, N., & Short-Camilli, C. (1995). *Bully-proofing your school: A comprehensive approach for elementary schools.* Longmont, CO: Sopris West.

Geneva, G. (1994). *At the essence of learning: Multicultural education.* West Lafayette, IN: Kappa Delta Pi.

Gibson, S., & Dembo, M. (1984). Teacher self-efficacy: A construct validation. *Journal of Educational Psychology, 76,* 569–582.

Goldstein, A. P. (1986). Psychological skills training and the aggressive adolescent. In S. J. Apter & A. P. Goldstein (Eds.), *Youth violence: Programs and prospects.* Oxford, England: Pergamon.

Goldstein, A. P. (1999). *The Prepare Curriculum: Teaching prosocial competencies* (rev. ed.). Champaign, IL: Research Press.

Goldstein, A. P., Glick, B., & Gibbs, J. C. (1998). *Aggression Replacement Training: A comprehensive intervention for aggressive youth* (rev. ed.). Champaign, IL: Research Press.

Goldstein, A. P., & McGinnis, E. (1997). *Skillstreaming the adolescent: New strategies and perspectives for teaching prosocial skills* (rev. ed.). Champaign, IL: Research Press.

Goldstein, A. P., & Michaels, G. Y. (1985). *Empathy: Development, training, and consequences.* Hillsdale, NJ: Erlbaum.

Gottheil, N. F. (1996, November). *Bullies and victims: Calibration of peer and self-reports.* Poster session presented at the 30th annual convention of the Association for Advancement of Behavior Therapy, New York.

Hargreaves, D. (1980). Teachers' knowledge of behavior problems. In G. Upton & A. Gobell (Eds.), *Behavior problems in the comprehensive school.* Cardiff, Wales: Faculty of Education, University College.

Hayes, R. L. (1995). Continuing to give psychology away. *Elementary School Guidance and Counseling, 30,* 155–159.

Hazler, R. J. (1996). *Breaking the cycle of violence: Interventions for bullying and victimization.* Washington, DC: Accelerated Development.

Holmes Group. (1986). *Tomorrow's trends: A report of the Holmes Group.* East Lansing: Michigan State University.

Hoover, J. H., & Hazler, R. J. (1991). Bullies and victims. *Elementary School Guidance and Counseling, 25,* 212–219.

Hoover, J. H., Oliver, R., & Hazler, R. J. (1992). Bullying: Perceptions of adolescent victims in the Midwestern USA. *School Psychology International, 13,* 5–16.

Horne, A. M. (1981). Aggressive behavior in normal and deviant members of intact versus mother-only families. *Journal of Abnormal Child Psychology, 9,* 283–290.

Horne, A. M. (1991). Social learning family therapy. In A. M. Horne & J. Passmore (Eds.), *Family counseling and therapy* (2nd ed.). Itasca, IL: Peacock.

Horne, A. M., Forehand, R., Norsworthy, K., & Frame. (1990). Behavioral approaches to couple and family therapy. In A. M. Horne & J. Passmore (Eds.), *Family counseling and therapy* (2nd ed.). Itasca, IL: Peacock.

Horne, A. M., Glaser, B., & Sayger, T. V. (1994). Bullies. *Counseling and Human Development, 27,* 1–12.

Horne, A. M., & Sayger, T. V. (1990). *Treating conduct and oppositional defiant disorders in children.* New York: Pergamon.

Horne, A. M. & Sayger, T. V. (2000). Behavioral approaches to couple and family therapy. In A. M. Horne (Ed.), *Family counseling and therapy* (3rd ed.). Itasca, IL: Peacock.

Horne, A. M., & Socherman, R. E. (1996). Profile of a bully. Who would do such a thing? *Educational Horizons, 74,* 77–83.

Horne, A. M., Socherman, R. E., & Dagley, J. (1998). *Teacher efficacy and attribution: A construct validation.* Unpublished manuscript, University of Georgia, Athens.

Hranitz, J. R., & Eddowes, E. A. (1990). Violence: A crisis in homes and schools. *Childhood Education, 66,* 4-7.

Huberty, C. J., DiStefano, C., & Kamphaus, R. W. (1996). Behavioral clustering of school children. *Multivariate Behavioral Research, 32,* 105–134.

Johnstone, M., Munn, P., & Edwards, L. (1991). *Action against bullying: Drawing from experience.* Edinburgh: Scottish Council for Research Education.

Jones, M. A., & Krisberg, B. (1994). *Images and reality: Juvenile crime, youth violence and public policy.* San Francisco: National Council on Crime and Delinquency.

Keppel, G. (1991). *Design and analysis: A researcher's handbook.* Upper Saddle River, NJ: Prentice Hall.

Kikkawa, M. (1987). Teachers' opinions and treatments for bully/victim problems among students in junior and senior high schools: Results of a fact-finding survey. *Journal of Human Development, 23,* 25–30.

Kreidler, W. (1984). *Creative conflict resolution: More than 200 activities for keeping peace in the classroom.* Glenview, IL: Scott Foresman.

Lee, F. (1993, April 4). Disrespect rules. *The New York Times Educational Supplement,* p. 16.

Lewis, J. A., & Lewis, M. D. (1983). *Community counseling: A human services approach* (2nd ed.). New York: Wiley.

Little, S. G., & White, K. (1996). *Implementing classroom interventions: The importance of teacher variables.* Unpublished manuscript, Northern Illinois University, DeKalb.

Loeber, R., & Dishion, T. J. (1984). Boys who fight at home and school: Family conditions influencing cross-setting consistency. *Journal of Consulting and Clinical Psychology, 52,* 759–768.

Lowenstein, J. S. (1978). A comparison of the self-esteem between boys living with single-parent mothers and single-parent fathers. *Journal of Divorce, 2,* 195–208.

Martin, R. P. (1988). *Assessment of personality and behavior problems.* New York: Guilford.

McGinnis, E., & Goldstein, A. P. (1997). *Skillstreaming the elementary school child: New strategies and perspectives for teaching prosocial skills* (rev. ed.). Champaign, IL: Research Press.

McGraw-Hill School Systems. (1994). *Osiris: Getting started.* Denver: Author.

McWhirter, J. J., McWhirter, B. T., McWhirter, A. M., & McWhirter, E. H. (1998). *At-risk youth: A comprehensive response* (2nd ed.). Pacific Grove, CA: Brooks/Cole.

Mellor, A. (1990). Bullying in Scottish secondary schools. *Spotlights, 23,* 1–8.

Minuchin, S. (1974). *Families and family therapy.* Cambridge, MA: Harvard University.

Minuchin, S. (1988). A systems perspective on development. In R. A. Hinde & J. Stevenson-Hinde (Eds.), *Relationships within families: Mutual influences.* Oxford, England: Clarendon Press.

Moran, S., Smith, P., & Thompson, D. (1993). Ethnic differences in experiences of bullying: Asian and White children. *British Journal of Educational Psychology, 63,* 431–440.

Mosher, R., & Sprinthall, N. A. (1971). Deliberate psychological education. *Counseling Psychologist, 2,* 3–82.

Munthe, E., & Roland, E. (1989). *Bullying: An international perspective.* London, England: David Fulton.

Newman, D. A. (1999). *The effectiveness of a psychoeducational intervention for classroom teachers aimed at reducing bullying behavior in middle school students.* Unpublished doctoral dissertation, University of Georgia, Athens.

Newman, D. A., & Horne, A. M. (in press). The effectiveness of a psychoeducational intervention for classroom teachers aimed at reducing bullying behavior in middle school students. *Professional School Counseling.*

Norsworthy, K., & Horne, A. M. (1994, July). *Social learning family therapy: An intervention and teaching model for families with aggressive children.* Paper presented at the International Conference on Family Psychology, Padua, Italy.

O'Donohue, W., & Krasner, L. (1995). Psychological skills training. In W. O'Donohue & L. Krasner (Eds.), *Handbook of psychological skills training: Clinical techniques and applications.* Boston: Allyn & Bacon.

Oja, S. N. (1979). Deliberate psychological education and its impact on teachers and students in a junior high school. *Humanist Educator, 18,* 64–73.

Oliver, R., Hoover, J. H., & Hazler, R. J. (1994). The perceived roles of bullying in small-town Midwestern schools. *Journal of Counseling and Development, 72,* 416–421.

Oliver, R., Oaks, I. N., & Hoover, J. H. (1994). Family issues and interventions in bully and victim relationships. *School Counselor, 4,* 199–202.

Olweus, D. (1978). *Aggression in the schools: Bullies and whipping boys.* Washington, DC: Hemisphere.

Olweus, D. (1993). Victimization by peers: Antecedents and long-term outcomes. In K. H. Rubin & J. B. Asendorf (Eds.), *Social withdrawal, inhibition, and shyness.* Hillsdale, NJ: Erlbaum.

Olweus, D. (1994). Annotation—Bullying at school: Basic facts and effects of a school based intervention program. *Journal of Child Psychology and Psychiatry, 35,* 1171–1190.

Pallas, A. M., Natriello, G., & Mcdell, E. L. (1995). *Changing students: Changing needs.* University of Chicago Press.

Patterson, G. R. (1982). *Coercive family process.* Eugene, OR: Castalia.

Patterson, G. R. (1986). Performance models for antisocial boys. *American Psychologist, 41,* 432–444.

Pellegrini, A. D. (1998). Bullies and victims in school: A review and call for research. *Journal of Applied Developmental Psychology, 19,* 165–176.

Perry, D. G., Kusel, S. J., & Perry, L. C. (1988). Victims of peer aggression. *Developmental Psychology, 24,* 807–814.

Pierce, K. A., & Cohen, R. C. (1995). Aggressors and their victims: Toward a contextual framework for understanding children's aggressor-victim relationships. *Developmental Review, 15,* 292–310.

Reynolds, C. R., & Kamphaus, R. W. (1992). *Behavior assessment system for children (BASC).* Circle Pines, MN: American Guidance Service.

Rigby, K., & Slee, P. (1991). Bullying among Australian school children: Reported behavior and attitudes toward victims. *Journal of Social Psychology, 131,* 615–627.

Rofes, E. E. (1994). Making our schools safe for sissies. *High School Journal, 77,* 37–40.

Roberts, W. B., Jr., & Coursol, D. H. (1996). Strategies for intervention with childhood and adolescent victims of bullying, teasing, and intimidation in school settings. *Elementary School Guidance and Counseling, 30,* 204–212.

Roland, E. (1989). A system oriented strategy against bullying. In E. Roland & E. Munthe (Eds.), *Bullying: An international perspective.* London: Professional Development Foundation.

Ross, D. M. (1996). *Childhood bullying and teasing: What school personnel, other professionals, and parents can do.* Alexandria, VA: American Counseling Association.

Sayger, T. V., Horne, A. M., Walker, J. M., & Passmore, J. L. (1988). Social learning family therapy with aggressive children: Treatment outcome and maintenance. *Journal of Family Psychology, 3,* 261–285.

Schrumpf, F., Crawford, D. K., & Bodine, R. J. (1997). *Peer mediation: Conflict resolution in schools* (rev. ed.). Champaign, IL: Research Press.

Shapiro, E. S., DuPaul, G. J., Bradley, K. L., & Bailey, L. T. (1996). A school-based consultation program for service delivery to middle school students with attention-deficit/hyperactivity disorder. *Journal of Emotional and Behavioral Disorders, 4,* 73–81.

Sharp, S., & Smith, P. K. (1991). Bullying in UK schools: The DES Sheffield bullying project. *Early Child Development and Care, 77,* 47–55.

Shaver, K. J. (1975). *An introduction to attribution processes.* Cambridge, MA: Winthrop.

Shure, M. B. (1992a). *I Can Problem Solve (ICPS): An interpersonal cognitive problem-solving program for children* (Preschool). Champaign, IL: Research Press.

Shure, M. B. (1992b). *I Can Problem Solve (ICPS): An interpersonal cognitive problem-solving program for children* (Kindergarten & Primary Grades). Champaign, IL: Research Press.

Shure, M. B. (1992c). *I Can Problem Solve (ICPS): An interpersonal cognitive problem-solving program for children* (Intermediate Elementary Grades). Champaign, IL: Research Press.

Siann, G., Callaghan, M., Glissov, P., Lockhart, R., & Rawson, L. (1994). Who gets bullied? The effect of school, gender and ethnic group. *Educational Research, 36,* 123–134.

Sickmund, M., Snyder, H. N., & Poe-Yamagata, E. (1997). *Juvenile offenders and victims: 1997 update on violence.* Washington, DC: Office of Juvenile Justice and Delinquency Prevention.

Slee, P., & Rigby, K. (1993). Australian school children's self appraisal of interpersonal relations: The bullying experience. *Child Psychiatry and Human Development, 23,* 273–282.

Smith, P., & Boulton, M. (1990). Rough and tumble play, aggression, and dominance: Perception and behavior in children's encounters. *Human Development, 33,* 271–282.

Smith P. K., & Sharp, S. (1994). *School bullying: Insights and perspectives.* London: Routledge and Kegan Paul.

Soodak, L. C., & Podell, D. M. (1994). Teachers' thinking about difficult-to-teach students. *Journal of Educational Research, 88,* 44–51.

Soodak, L. C., & Podell, D. M. (1996). Teacher efficacy: Toward the understanding of a multi-faceted construct. *Teaching and Teacher Education, 12,* 401–411.

Stephenson, P., & Smith, D. (1987). Anatomy of the playground bully. *Education, 18,* 236–237.

Stephenson, P., & Smith, D. (1989). Bullying in the junior high. In D. P. Tattum & D. A. Lane (Eds.), *Bullying in schools.* Stoke-on-Trent, England: Trentham Books.

Tattum, D. P. (1989). Violence and aggression in schools. In D. P. Tattum & D. A. Lane (Eds.), *Bullying in schools.* Stoke-on-Trent, England: Trentham.

Trickett, E. J., & Moos, R. H. (1995). *Classroom environment scale manual: Development, applications, research* (3rd ed.). Palo Alto: Consulting Psychologists Press.

Turpeau, A. M. (1998). *Effectiveness of an anti-bullying classroom curriculum intervention on an American middle school.* Unpublished doctoral dissertation, University of Georgia, Athens.

Weber, B. J., & Omotani, L. M. (1994). The power of believing. *The Executive Educator, 19,* 35-38.

Wiggins, J. S., & Winder, C. L. (1961). The Peer Nomination Inventory: An empirically derived sociometric measure of adjustment in preadolescent boys. *Psychological Reports, 9,* 643–677.

Whitney, I., Rivers, I., Smith, P. K., & Sharp, S. (1994). In P. K. Smith & S. Sharp (Eds.), *School bullying: Insights and perspectives.* London: Routledge and Kegan Paul.

Wilezenski, F. L., Steegman, R., Braun, M., Feeley, F., Griffin, J., Horowitz, T., & Olson, S. (1994). *Promoting "fair play": Interventions for children as victims and victimizers.* (ERIC Document Reproduction Service No. ED 380 744)

Woolfolk, A. E., Rosoff, B., & Hoy, W. K. (1990). Teachers' sense of efficacy and their beliefs about managing students. *Teaching and Teacher Education, 6,* 137–148.

Young, G. H. (1994). *Developing students' knowledge, intervention skills, and willingness to participate in decreasing school bullying: A secondary school's use of the curriculum approach.* (ERIC Document Reproduction Service No. ED 379 538)

About the Authors

Dawn Newman-Carlson, Ph.D., a health psychologist, is the president of Carlson Health Promotion, P.A., a counseling and consulting corporation, with her primary practice located in Jacksonville, Florida. She earned her doctorate in counseling psychology at the University of Georgia, completed a clinical residency at the Medical College of Georgia, specializing in pediatric psychology, and a postdoctoral fellowship in pediatric health psychology at the University of Florida. Dawn was the co-developer and program administrator of the Bully Prevention Project. Since 1995, she has worked on developing, refining, and implementing the project. As a consultant, she trains school personnel and counselors in the areas of childhood aggression and bully prevention. She works with families and school systems to create lifestyles that promote health and self-esteem for children and adolescents. Dawn conducts *Bully Busters* training workshops for schools across the country and has been invited to present the *Bully Busters* program at national conferences. Her research and publications concern prevention and early intervention for bullies and victims, health promotion, disease prevention, diabetes, and adherence.

Arthur M. "Andy" Horne, Ph.D., is distinguished research professor at the University of Georgia. He received his Ph.D. from Southern Illinois University in 1971 and completed a postdoctoral clinical research internship in 1987–1988. He taught at Indiana State University from 1971 until 1989, where he served as a member of the faculty and director of training for the counseling psychology program, as well as a member of the marriage and family therapy training program. In 1988, Andy joined the faculty of the University of Georgia, serving as director of training for and head of the Department of Counseling and Human Development Services as well as coordinator of a certificate program in marriage and family therapy. He is a fellow of four divisions of the American Psychological Association (APA), past president of the Association for Specialists in Group Work, past president of the Division of Group Psychology and Group Psychotherapy of the APA, former editor of the *Journal for Specialists in Group Work* and the *International Journal for the Advancement of Counselling*. He has coauthored five books, coedited four, and served on the editorial boards of seven journals. Research on violence reduction and bully/victim interventions is a primary focus of his work. Currently, Andy is involved with ACT EARLY, a program funded by the U.S. Department of Education's Office of At-Risk Children to identify effective teacher interventions for children at risk for emotional and behavioral problems, and the GREAT Schools and Families Project for reducing aggression in middle schools, funded by the Centers for Disease Control and Prevention, and coordinates the Bully Prevention Project of the College of Education at the University of Georgia. Andy enjoys travel and conducts workshops and training on bullying and reducing aggression in families and schools in the United States and abroad.

Christi L. Bartolomucci, Ph.D., a licensed psychologist, is co-director of Kids On The Move, a comprehensive center for children and adolescents specializing in ADHD, located in Atlanta. Her primary services include child, adolescent, and family therapy and psychological assessment. She also has ongoing interests in consultation and program development. Christi received her doctoral degree in counseling psychology from the University of Georgia. She completed a clinical child internship at the University of Louisville and a postdoctoral fellowship in pediatric psychology at Emory University in Atlanta. Since 1997, Christi has been actively involved with the Bully Prevention Project, a team effort committed to better understanding and addressing childhood bullying and victimization, childhood aggression, and promoting the healthy development of children.